PONY WISDOM FOR THE SOUL

Pony Wisdom
for the Soul

C. Norman Shealy, M.D., Ph.D.

2008
Galde Press, Inc.
Lakeville, Minnesota, U.S.A.

First Edition
First Printing, 2008

Cover painting by Crawford
Cover design by Christopher Wells
Sketches by Scott Farmer

Galde Press, Inc.
PO Box 460
Lakeville, Minnesota 55044–0460
www.galdepress.com

Introduction

Several years ago I had the great fortune of being introduced to a quite remarkable woman, who has chosen quietly to be a mentor to many, with far less public acknowledgment than the average grade-school teacher. She has provided me with more answers to important existential questions than any of the world-renowned philosophers.

She has asked to remain anonymous. Indeed, I only received permission to write her story when I suggested that royalties would all go to her favorite charity, Personal Ponies, Ltd. In order to discuss her philosophy, I have chosen to call her Dolly and to use the symbol of a pony, Muffy, as the teacher. This is an allegory in the time-honored sense. Out of the mouths of the innocent shall come the truth.

Horses have long been the archetype of freedom, symbols of consciousness and all of nature. The pony as the innocent child represents essential wisdom.

The essence of her knowledge has been suggested in Buddhism and Hinduism, elaborately expounded in A *Course In Miracles* and in longer books attempting to summarize that work. Muffy's message cuts to the truth in few words. I have been the scribe, summarizing her message, culled from well over a thousand pages of correspondence. You might say I was a slow learner, asking the same question over and over. The answer was consistently simple and to the point:

This is a dream. There is no time. Forgive all. Love. *Awaken* to the reality of Heaven.

Some years ago I asked another guide, "What percent of people are conscious?" The answer was "Six percent."

That of course raises the question of "What is conscious?"

Muffy would say it is being "Awake." This suggests that not being awake is unconscious, similar to our state of sleep. And if ninety-four percent of people are asleep, then surely the world is but a dream. To sleep, perchance to dream? And if all of our so-called life is a dream, then what is real?

I invite you to listen to Muffy!

Pony Wisdom for the Soul

Albert Einstein wrote in his book The World As I See It *that the harmony of natural law: Reveals an intelligence of such superiority that, compared with it, all the systematic thinking and acting of human beings is an utterly insignificant reflection.*

Four million years ago, a vast circle of light in a field of dreams began an evolutionary journey as an angelic, energetic being. This light began the inevitable journey into physical form as we know it and eventually earned a life on Erra, a life of quiet and joy, long and long in school and long and long amid the Galactic Council learning the ways of the immortals.

Erra is a planet in the Pleiades, 580 light years away from us but shifted a fraction of time ahead of our space-time dimension.

Seven hundred seventy-five earth years ago, on the peaceful planet Erra, Anah was born to a life of peaceful study. Then just seventy-five years ago came a call from Qua "Anah (On-Ah), the doll house of earth beacons. Go forth from seven hundred years of becoming."

"Yes," answered Anah. And soon Dolly was born to a family in New York State. These are the recollections of the early life of Dolly.

⊶ ⊷

At four months of age a messenger comes. The messenger is "Qua," inter-world traveler. A tiny figure in blue, lisle stockings and satin slippers, pearl-seeded trousers and jacket, who landed lightly on my four-month old right leg as I lay awake in the new pram Grandmother bought for me. Qua wrote my past in lightning strokes on my infant brain, and the lessons of lifetimes held steady, as their pages were impressed there, never to be forgotten. The blue-shirted traveler sailed through the open window as the south wind blew the white cotton curtains apart, allowing his outbound journey to universes beyond. Pale peach and blue figures on the inside hood of my pram seared my infant eyes. I would remember. I would indeed remember. I do remember.

Dream 000185654559
Dolly

Age four and a visit with cousins to a village church. The unbaptized are not fit for receiving the bread they passed close before my huge brown eyes as I sat on the pew, entranced by the white robes and sweet voices of a choir singing "Jesus Loves Me This I Know." Once home I placed by head under the water pump and sang "Jesus Loves Me." Baptized now? Presentable now?

"Ah, no," I was told.

———— ⚔ ————

Age four and the huge pillared farmhouse was afire. Mama, sister, and baby brother were napping. Gray snowflakes landed on the driveway where I sat barefoot and cross-legged while counting and doing subtraction with stones. (This I was allowed to do each afternoon instead of sleeping.) I looked up, and pushing my brown bathrobe around my scrawny self, ran barefoot up the back stairs and shook Mama's shoulder. "It's raining gray snowflakes, big ones and they are so pretty!" She reached for my baby brother beside her and I took my little sister's hand. We flew down the stairs and out toward the stable as the roof of the east wing where they were sleeping caved in with a mighty roar. My nap time counting stones surely saved our lives.

Age four and a half: I worked for Grandmother all summer and saved ten pennies. My coveted diamond ring in Kresges' Five and Ten-Cent store was waiting for me. At last, all mine! Little sister dropped my precious diamond ring in the maw of the floor heat register and I could hear it pinging its way down, down, down. I wanted to scream but did not. Instead, I comforted little sister and cried not a tear for my deep loss.

Age four and a half: My pet turkey Gertrude scraped off her breast feathers when she flew from the upstairs porch to the asphalt below. Lovingly Grandmother taped a cheesecloth bandage across Gertrude's ample front and it looked for all the world like a big white bib. I was pleased to tears over her caring about my pet.

Age six, lying in a field of Indian paintbrushes: the red and orange flowers dimply and swaying as the breeze blew their heads now this way and that. I watched a no-nonsense gray striped field spider spin her warrior-best-silken threads with the hope of catching her dinner or next day's lunch. Carefully she ranged between the paintbrushes, endlessly working, struggling, and swinging her round-bellied body over and over toward a distant stem. Success was hers. Lesson indeed as I lay there: Never allow failure to be real.

Age nine: Holding a small, wild lavender aster, or was it a blue cornflower? My voyage into the land of becoming; my graduation to what is real. This is fantasy and these forms, these shapes, these trees and these rocks. This is not their real self. This earth-life is but a pantomime dance. This is not it! Here we learn our lines and dash on stage and off again. It's a dreamdance and we are the performers.

Age thirteen and my own carefully constructed vow, very like the gray-striped spider that insisted on accomplishing her web-spinning spell to insure groceries for supper would soon arrive. "I hereby refuse to accept anything that is not success! I refuse to accept that which I am told about religion and God and human history in books. It's not that way! That which I am learning; that which is being presented to me as real, it is not real. This I know and can never, ever be dissuaded." That is the vow I carefully recorded in my leather notebook as I sat under my favorite pine tree those many years ago, wartime, summer of 1944.

But how to live in a world that is not what it seems? Be an atheist. That's the road less traveled.

I will spend my life seeking the one, if there is a one, making a realness of what is, not the world that appears to me. I must meet that one, if it exists. Then of course, there follows the important question. A whole life of seeking? And, at the end, if there is no maker of the real? Reasoned as carefully as possible at age thirteen, "It will not matter. It will not matter because dead is dead."

As dead as that little star-nose mole near my left foot? That little point of light no longer squeaking in his soft gray-mole skin is simply a non-squeaking mole. His body to disintegrate into what looks like earth but is really little silver light twinkles very like sparklers on the Fourth of July? Mole no longer? Me no longer?

⊷ ⊱✦⊰ ⊶

Age fifteen: The art room and my drawing of a pony beneath an apple tree is required. Mine was inadequate, which was not unusual, however, as the teacher reached to crumple my drawing and ask for better, I said "No, No! This means something, I must keep it!" My brother, age thirteen, died that day of epilepsy and his brown magical pony, a harness strap from the stable, (he called it "Kate,") died with him. Forty years later the magical kingdom of real Shetland "Kate Ponies" began their parade into the hearts of kids who are differently able, touching lives at the trot: Personal Ponies, Ltd.

But back to age thirteen:

And then came Muffy

Dear sweet Muffy: twenty-four inches of black Shetland, brilliant and so incredibly aware. Muffy is formally known as Greystone Little Miss Muffet and neither spiders nor anything else ever frightens her in anyway whatever. When she was born as thirteen inches short, Cornet Vets came to make sure she was fine and could not find her in the stall. We walked back to the stall with others and said, "There she is, right there." They thought she was a little pile of manure that her dam was standing over. One vet put her in his coat pocket.

Muffy's Papa (barely thirty inches) showed in hand in the mixed MT/Moorland Stallion Class and stood reserve to a cob, "Bryan Casey." He barely came to the cob's knee and had just as much bone as the cob! The English judge asked how we ever managed to get the boy out of England as he should have remained. We said we found him in a cornfield in Illinois. She did not know what to say, so remarked that he was certainly a fine lad. Life is amusing, yes?

Soon Dolly and Muffy began a conversation on the meaning of life on earth. With perfect intuitive connections the two entered a fifteen-year dialogue.

Muffy: You see, Dolly, you and I are all part of the greatest dream known, the dream of life on planet earth. People are not ready to admit this, not even to begin to understand the major lesson that life is all a great dream. But you can, and perhaps you can help me explain this so that the children will understand.

⸺ ⸭ ⸺

Dolly: But who is dreaming, Muffy?

Muffy: You are, my friend, all of us are on a great stage.

You are "Dolly of the dream." Your life in this dream is of excruciating importance to "Dolly of the dream," and you and your work are equally, excruciatingly important to your family, your friends, your child admirers, and your world. Take nothing from this life you are choosing. Herald it, exalt it, and be proud of it. But make no mistake, Dolly, its importance is within the dream itself. It's not important to your life in Heaven as the one created and beloved of God. You need no record of success with God. God loves you. There is nothing more to say except God loves you. You need no more resumé than that. You are indeed a dream figure on a dream stage in a dream world that you are making in the moment. Yes, and all the probable, possible, parallel, nearly endless universes of dream, Dolly, that are imaginable. Yes, you are a dream figure on those dream stages too.

All your dreams are planned carefully. Your every moment is planned carefully. Awake or dreaming it is just that your conscious self, Dolly in person, does not recollect what is going on. That takes practice.

◆—◆ ⊠✦⊠ ◆—◆

Dolly: Even Jonathan Swift, who is one of the greatest multifaceted writers, could not create a plot with six billion people, plus trillions of other props.

Muffy: In the shape and image of Jonathan Swift as human, most likely he would find it difficult if not impossible to have nearly infinite plots, true enough.

However, Jonathan Swift, as is true of each one of us, is not just "Jonathan Swift Human/Writer," no matter how talented in his human form.

Without a doubt, Jonathan Swift is a multifaceted personality with nearly infinite numbers of Jonathan Swifts in various guises and alternate names in all the lives and phantom and parallel, possible or probable lifetimes imaginable. We are dwellers of now; Dolly, and that means, as you know, that all we could possibly dream is now, this instant. All the guises are now a lot of information and material for a human brain. Not impossible perhaps, but mighty weighty?

Let go of the idea of limitation. Let go of the idea of time. Let go of the idea of the "scarcity principle." If you allow yourself to let go of your belief that dream universes are limited, and they are not limited, then all things are possible under this sun or any other.

You dreamed up the Dolly of your dreams. You dreamed the stage play and actors on your dream stage, whether they be ETs, Ranthian, New Yorkers, Appaloosa, or come from Arkansas. You are dreaming your dream. You are the dreamer. You are the dreamer who plans, blueprints, executes, enjoys, laments, dances, smiles, and cries over the dream you are dreaming. You the dreamer of all Dolly dreams!

You, the multifaceted dreamer. You, the playwright. You, the determiner of your journey, and with you are the actors who agree to join you on your journey to wherever you the dreamer chooses to take yourself. Dear one, it's your dream. Anyone or anything that seems to be in the focus of Dolly is placed there by you with agreement from those who seem to be there with you. We are all just some dream of enormous proportions, true unimaginable proportions. It is very true but a dream it is.

Are we not doing just that? Muffy embracing and executing her dream ideas in her dream world each moment. Is not the Dolly I seem to know embracing and executing her book

Dream 001184134154
Dolly

to the dream world in a way that has to indicate to anyone who encounters you that your ideas and your family and your plans are indeed embraced and executed and offered to one and all if they are interested? Is that not proof enough that at least this Dolly of this day is up and at her business of embracing and executing?

It's all the proof that dreams can offer, Dolly. Your school book lying there on your lovely chaise in your living room is certainly the corpus of your dream. Agreed? You are doing it. Are you so close to the action that you cannot see the action that embraces and executes?

Remember, too, that ego is never satisfied. Ego never really wants answers. Ego wants questions to continue on and on. This keeps ego alive and well and checking out the next season's greeting cards.

⸻ ⬦ ⸻

Dolly: And does the dream never end?

Muffy: We dream endlessly until, and the until is when we decide to dream no more. That's when we are home where we never left and you, as will everyone, will hear the echoed, joyful laugh of eternity that translated means: "Oh, I did seem to go out and dream my dreams." My imaginings of what seemed to me composed of an awesome splendor even I cannot comprehend. I did, yes I did, of so many times of glory and defeat. The times of treasure, the times of agony and the times of rising to mountaintops. Yes, now, by golly, yes! Amazing that I gather my dreams to me and understand that those were merely the times of dreams, nothing more.

All is illusion, dream generated out of my desire to be me, *moi*, and to offer who I am to any who would care to dwell with me a time. But yes, now I see all is made up, all that glory and agony, defeat and success, and all that rivalry. All that was but dream; my own productions. So that's what I have been doing, wandering about in dreams, planning my days and nights without ceasing. Making dreams that even I neglected to remember were mine. Ah, me, and here I am back home having this realization, oh, so, pleased with myself over my productions and yet glad, glad, so glad that they are less than the nothing of mare's tails clouds, the downy feathers on a chick, the white furze of blossoms on tupelo trees, the distant thump of an X in a forest, the rise and fall of a barometer. The minuteness of one molecule. Here I am no longer dreaming and how happy I am to be home, oh yes, home.

—— ·+×÷×+· ——

Dolly: And even Erra is a dream?

Muffy: I share what I know but I am certain it is scanty compared to what others might know about our past. Your emphasis was reporting to and being involved with the Galactic Council, not interplanetary that I know of, but between what I think are the five planets in the Taurus constellation. You may have been involved with the Intergalactic Council but I do not actually remember that as being so. I do know that earth humans are a mixed tribe from many galaxies and different dimensions. I think I can offer more on this at some point. Probably not a whole lot, but certainly some.

Dolly: And we really choose all this, Muffy?

Muffy: We choose to be here in a dream world on dream stages. Yes, it is a dream choice and it is our dream choice and we are not real as the personalities we firmly believe are real. Our egos refuse to accept that we dream. In Heaven Dolly has no name, no personality even faintly like the Dolly I am getting to know in her dream world. This Dolly I am dreaming is a made-up person in my script and on my stage of my choosing, life just as Muffy is dreamed by all the many others who put this Muffy on their stages in their dream lives in this now.

There is no world out there. It is all make believe. All is mind, and ideas do not leave their creative artist author. What we think of as a world is a projection from our minds. You are your own dream, and you are in my dream and those of all others who know you. We are all dream figures in one another's dreams. We act out our parts on stages in a dream world or in many dream worlds. When we awaken to the fact that we are dreaming, we laugh! Then we smile a lot and we live outwardly in a manner that is dignified and seemingly real. We do it with panache and kindness and as much truth as we can muster, all the while knowing we are dreaming. That is enlightenment. We laugh some more at ourselves, knowing we are safely in a heaven we never left, perfect as God's creation.

Dolly: Muffy, is there any purpose to this "life?"

Muffy: This dream world and any others have no purpose whatsoever. It serves as a way for the dream self-ego to insist on its separation from its source, God, and to hide because of the guilt of choosing an ego. *A Course in Miracles* puts it well. We forgot to laugh at the tiny, mad idea that such could actually happen. We are not here and neither is anything else; there is no purpose, as we never left heaven. The universe is yours. The way it goes is the way you truly want it regardless of what appears in writing, in green things, and in conscious understanding. You are the guides. Guide your thoughts to your intent and allow, allow, allow what comes down.

Dolly: Where does ego stop?

Muffy: It does not stop in this level if given a paddock to own. It races about, looking full of itself and hoping everyone will notice. If ego is taken for what it is, a shadow, a shade, a nothing that suits this level but has no breadth nor depth nor heft, there are no qualities for admiring. And, if one presses its slithery self to the wall and beyond, it admits its failure as "one who is not" and reckons itself to be what it is, a mere nothing. What comes forth is a glad and accepting whole that takes what is and smiles and says, "Ah, in the dream world scheme of things what is what is and that too fades into the world of gray dandelions blown away by the sly north wind. And, some sort of grand ideal set in? Your grand ideal is set in dandelion seeds and will either find its ground for growing or will scatter and be what it all is anyway, a non-place, in a non-reality, in an illusion we want to call real." Being neither grand nor small, lift your spirit into the idea of it all. Smile a lot and take what comes to you.

God loves creation, us. We are like God, but we are not God. We are the created. We are happy together as one in heaven. We are seemingly here in three dimensions and we think it is real. It is not real. Only Heaven is real. This dream you are living and each one of us is living, myriad lives all in this now. Dream. Not true! Discernment, the ability to see beyond the obvious. The ability to find the best way to resolve that which is needful of attention in the moment. Discernment is a skill learned by making errors in judgment. As Maya Angelou tells us, "We do the best we know to do and when we know better, we do better."

——— ‡‡ ‡≡ ‡ ———

Dolly: And time, Muffy?

Muffy: All is now. All of anything that ever happens in nothingness is this instant. All universes, galaxies, thoughts, images, forms, anything we call something is made up. All is in a nanosecond. There is no time except as we who use brains use time as a tool. Time exists because we make it so. We use time in a linear fashion. It is not the way of things.

Yes, we all do that. Choosing illusion each second we are seemingly here in this illusionary place we call our life on planet earth. We are choosing illusion. We firmly believe this is real; denying that is so is of no use whatever. We do believe it is so! We are intensely and firmly ensconced in this level of what we call our dear and deeply embraced life in three dimensions. We may give intellectual agreement in great, hulking sentences; we may give verbal weight to our understanding that this is not real, but actually believing what we say is quite another matter and very, very difficult. We do not believe ourselves in those statements. So it's best to just live our best and be Mona Lisa. It is more honest.

Dolly: Do I stop a process of growth and enlightenment by allowing ego its run of attachments and beliefs in that moment?

Muffy: Certainly not. You have that moment of realizing the depth and intensity of your choosing! As we all do, it is typical of anyone who sees the difference yet clings to that which we seem to know so well. Blood and guts and sinews and treadmills and fuzzy pony manes, dear friends' smiles and those whom we love in bodies that we can hug on occasion!

⤖✠⤗

Dolly: What about our attachments to others in our dream? Do we have to non-attach even from (or especially from) loved ones?

Muffy: The answer is all tough stuff, asking not less than everything, as it says in the Dickens story of "Little Giddings." All that we seem to hold dear in such a typical and startling, innocent manner must be allowed its value: nothing. Zero. Nada. In its place is transformation to everything eternal, non-transitory, changeless. It is a tall order expected of us who seem to be so lacking in the ability to let go. Yet it is happening all over the planet, eons' worth.

It can start with deeply focused inner eyes, as if one's fingers are pressing through stone as though it was something like a croissant. Laugh in the moment at the antics and the jokes we play on ourselves as we hug our "worldly garments so tightly." And Hawkins says, do it lightly and loosely. You go right on accepting the inner intersections of your holy and sacred mind, teaching you that "things are not as they seem." You smile and giggle and laugh at the silly treadmill, the quacking ducks, the umbrella that refuses to open, the finger caught in the door latch, the aroma of Richard's supper, the crunch of your salad, the fit of your jeans, the wiggle in your toes. You smile at yourself knowing it is not so and you go for lunch and listen to a friend, you swim in your glorious tiled pool, you straighten the curtain in that lovely room. You pause a moment looking out at the gate. You see within and you do what is needed.

Remember the horrors? It is so hard to see what we love torn into shreds of nothingness, torn and wrapped asunder. Our hearts recoil and say, "Oh, my God, no, no!" Do not ask it. Yet, God had nothing whatever to do with our terrors, our squirming, our tears and screams. We make them ours by believing in them and by making them up in the moment and then lamenting what we are making, though not believing we are doing it.

The only way out of such a muddle is to realize we make what we experience. We can unmake it and we must. Then and only then can that which is grand and perfect and wonderful beyond wonderful fill us with its perfection. Letting go is like being given your very first helium balloon at age two and watching a breeze blow it to the pear tree in the neighbor's yard where it tears itself on a branch. It's no longer your treasure, your very own, very special gift. It is gone, changed and not the same at all. Ah, the hot tears, the wishing and the disbelief. Oh, the kicking and screaming or the huge tear on a two-year-old cheek or the "Mommy/Daddy! Fix it!"

Life is letting go, and as those veils fly away those obstacles to your inner self leave you for that which is steadfast and enduring. A burning and intense desire to have it so makes a conflagration within. St. John of the Cross called it the dark night of the soul. Make no mistake, it is a death to the wee, small self and an awakening and a life to that which has lain hidden. Yes, we are all attached. If we were not, we would be long gone from this seeming earth spot.

Indeed, why not be happy? We make our reality. We make what we experience. We choose happy over being right or morose or dismal or deplorable. Of course choose happy. However, this is not a happy dimension. This is not a happy dream most of the time. Let's get real. Stuff happens a lot in this level. Love does not run this planet, not this galaxy nor this universe. It is made of nothingness. It is not eternal and it is not heaven. We choose to make it what it is. We choose to perpetrate this level of dream so we can be individual. Yet, we were created as one, not separate. We love our individuality. We love our separateness. We would not seem to be here if we did not. So we accept all the less than perfect. We make just so we can believe that our lives here are real and important. They are a dream.

⚜

Dolly: But why are people not happy? They choose problems?

Muffy: Happy is the best choice, for sure, but let's realistically look carefully at what is: death and taxes and sorrow and wars and all the other aspects of what we are doing to one another to keep the dream going. Egos prevail and we want it that way! My program was crafted to say, let's think differently. So is your work. So is the work of others. We act on the idea of doing this dimension better. That does not make it better but it is a better way to approach the dream in which we find ourselves. It makes us feel as though we are doing something positive and helpful, and gives us a moral and caring standard. Some do not care. We do care! The real idea is to change our minds about the world and to forgive everything because it never happened and is not happening. It is a dream.

We need to forgive every tiny aspect of our collaborative dream because it is a dream and never took place. It is not taking place and could not take place. We are dreaming together to keep individuality alive and well and thriving. That is the way to change the world. Look at the moment with a smile and

offer one's moments for doing service to others. Therefore, our
offerings are offered to self because we are all one. And then
leave the dream one day as being what it is, a dream, knowing
at that very moment we are in Heaven where we have ever been
and where we never left. It is as it is and we believe "it" thor-
oughly as being reality. As such we better do what we know to
be our best choices in the moments we seem to be living. Yes.
We can choose happy.

⊷ ⊨✛⊨ ⊶

Dolly: Can we just create happy?

Muffy: We are creative dreamers and we are creative! If a
bit more magic enables you to work out your dream in a way
that you want it to go, who is to say no? Only you. Drop the
belief in magic and you do not need it, but if you are unable in
the moment to drop that belief in magic, and replace it with
one that is not magic then use magic until you can work out a
better way. It's all your dream!

Magic in every step and is one better this morning? If so,
then you see it is magic at work! If not, repeat the magic or try
different magic and all the time you are working out your inner
beliefs about what you really want in your dream; a better way,
a more in-depth look at what is going on, a realization that you
truly do make your reality and what you have accomplished in

front of your eyes, etc. Keep ever in mind that it's far less important that outward manifestations show you have "fixed something" than it is to have inner realizations that are clear and
concise, i.e., you and you alone make your dream. Your mind
projects outwardly how successful you are at getting the inner
understanding of the artistry and creativity you possess as a
human in three dimensions.

Change your mind about your dream and your dream
changes. It has to, as you are its author. If you write a poem
called "Life," and you write it one way then that is your poem.
If you erase and change and add new lines and substitute new
words and add different punctuation, your poem called "Life"
is changed. That is exactly what your creative dream is, a series
of poems that you are constantly rearranging, improving, seeing more, understanding more, adding and subtracting and
sculpting your "Life Masterpiece." If that is where you are in
sculpting your "Dream Masterpiece," then recognize that it is
so and continue to sculpt and scour and scrub and smile as you
make it your own, which it is!

You are of the generation of what is called "silents" with
introspection, pre-indigo in understanding, being insightful,
aware and tuned to that frequency. Yes! All, however, are that.
We do not all peek toward the arena of insightfulness at the same
moment. All, however, are capable of exquisite understanding
and awareness. Hawkins insists when using his scale of one to

ten that we are in a way stopped up at the level that muscle test-
ing indicates. It is my premise that his test indicates this focused
lifetime only. And we live all lifetimes now. If there is a test for
each lifetime, I think findings about each one of us would bog-
gle the mind! As for genius, each in turn is genius. We do not all
realize genius is ours at the same moment. It is there; however,
most of us turn to other interests and other ways to live our
dream. Thus, my conclusion is that all are insightful, all are
geniuses at different moments in space/time/lifetimes.

Yes, it's the cover-up story that few ever admit to and fewer
still allow for daylight to show its morning face on that enormous mass belief. However, it is a mass belief and it is the basis
for all fears and all illness and all guilt! The enormity of our
guilt and shame and conviction that we are prodigals and have
attacked God by running and hiding in a world of our own
making is the very core of three dimensions and the ambigu-
ity of duality. We can choose our moments and laugh at God,
who did not allow for separate choices and individual intent
when perfection created perfection. We laugh and cry at one
and the same time. Here we are, believing we are individual and
separate standing atop a mountain that most of us believes God
made. And, we are required to live the commandments God
supposedly set for us and our guilt is there for not living up to
"God's Rules." On the other hand, here we are atop a mountain
of our own making and being at one and the same time happy
to be individual and unique and guilty and fearful to be found

out. So we hide here and quake in our boots that God will punish us for transgressions, and at the same time we pound our chests and say: "Ah ha, here I am, by golly. Now I like this individual idea and you, God, did not think of it; I did. It is I who invented an unlimited idea of who I am. Yet, God, I am afraid." Someone once said, "The degree to which each one of us awakens is in direct proportion to the amount of truth we can accept about ourselves!"

Dolly: And is there a beginning of awareness?

Muffy: A beginning. Catch the moment. Be aware of you in your body. In catching the moment, quite often it is a help to have a mantra, a word or a saying. Anything is fine to remind you that you are indeed awake and aware in that moment in your body. You say the word, mantra, or poem sound in your mind (it can be aloud, but usually it is not helpful). Because we are in duality, words do help. They can be any fragment, or anything really, that gives you a kind of anchor for your awake moment. Sit up straight now, and be aware of the length and width of you. Feel your eyes reading this page. Feel your backside on the chair. Feel your innerself as it reads these words and feel your awareness and awakeness, very much the you of you. That is what you are aiming for each moment, no matter what you are doing. That is the ultimate goal: to stay awake.

Forgiveness is understanding that nothing ever happened. That dreams of any kind are dreams, illusions, and then we laugh and laugh at ourselves for thinking otherwise!

⊷ ⊱⊰ ⊶

Dolly: How could we teach people to use their imagination or dreams to reach understanding to assist waking up?

Muffy: Ah, Dolly. The big catch question always asked by some well-intentioned professor in some dusty classroom, usually to undergraduates who scoff and think they have all the pertinent answers already! Dolly, I have no answers that are satisfactory. I can offer the following:

1. Readiness: That's step one. If an individual in some setting offers verbally (spoken or unspoken) a discontent with what it is, then perhaps one can offer in return the question, "What is it you find non-satisfying about your present belief system that gives you pause?" If, and it's a big if, there is a further question such as, "What would you like to change in your life at this time?" (the setting would need to be one of ease and lacking in intensity) Reply could lead to discussion and recommendation of a book, additional discussion, etc. "Reading readiness" for any change at any level in any area of communication of any kind whatever is crucial.

2. Awakening is usually a gradual process. For me it was instantaneous; that is neither preferred nor expected nor needful. It simply was so. The notion was given to reconsider any and all so-called assumptions. I did that in what could be called a flash of lightning." I got it, simply got it. The true "Ah, ha!" moment. I was very young, perhaps not carrying ingrained and determined beliefs at that age. You will do the same, Dolly.

3. There has to be at least a little willingness to consider a concept radically different from what has been assumed to that moment, with the presentation of an alternate concept. The natural way of things is that one considers, ponders, rejects, reconsiders, ponders again and again and gradually an expanded viewpoint that not only considers but embraces what appears as another, better way.

The curtains on the stage of dreams have been widened, pressed back and pushed further into the wings of time and space and one begins to see that there is more, so much more, than previously accepted. That is the usual process for changing one's mind about life, death, and taxes!

4. If there is application of an idea that is new, different, unusual, arresting, interesting, or intriguing mentally, it often follows there is additional seeking for more information. If that is the case, one offers only that quietly and with no fanfare. A suggestion, a recommended reading, written ideas, whatever might induce the questioner to proceed further into the quest that the questioner is ready to pursue and possibly at some point see as their own.

5. To answer your question personally, you will start teaching at age fourteen. You will quickly learn that a student who is passionately interested in learning is the proverbial "piece of cake!" Many years later you will have a cello student, age six, who simply swallows, digests, and reaches out for more and more information as fast as you can compile what she needs into a form that she can use at her age level.

The majority of students come to a teacher with all manner of attitudes, ranging from outright disdain to intense interest, and always a few like little Sophie Pauo who will play her tiny cello with all the verve and intensity of a Rostopovich! You know all this, Dolly. You will teach all your life.

6. When the time is right, and who knows when that is, the apple falls, the roast is ready, the foal is born, the blossom is open, and the tadpole becomes a frog. Awakening occurs when one reaches a point in time when an individual is simply ready to hear, consider, and embrace a better way. Every true teacher knows when that moment is happening. A foundation is laid that allows for what is to follow. This is your foundation, Dolly.

Dolly: What is God like?

Muffy: In absolute honesty, I confess I do not know! Having said that, however, I can offer the following as a way of approaching what is impossible to put into words while still in the dualistic dream-state using a physical body.

God is God. God has no opposite. Thus, there is no opposite to perfection because God is perfection. The nature of God is that which goes beyond any words used to describe the nature of the perfection that God is. Based on many years of teachings, when encountering the realm of purity and excellence, which is the very center of being, one loses all consciousness, place, substance, time, space, form, or image of any kind whatsoever. One becomes awareness. That is not a description. One becomes awareness!

It is often the word "light" that is used to attempt to convey that which is not possible to convey in words. That is not it. Perception, which is the position of our dualistic dream-self, is unable except in the briefest of moments to be free enough to grasp the tiniest of fragments of what is meant by eternal, changeless, utter life. Those moments of extreme brevity are quite simply great grace and allow the experience to return to dream-self with an awareness that never subsides. It never dulls. It never is other than a stamp on the core of being. One is sealed in every possible way with the stamp of eternity, eternity being utter life.

The above statement, though said with great honesty, is still perception expressed through the personality character of one who is invited to experience a glimpse. It is, as to be expected, said by an actor on a stage in the dream where we believe we stand and relate our lines to whomever has an interest in approximate words that in truth are basically meaningless.

Life is Heaven. God is Heaven. We are one with God in that Heaven. It is done. It has ever been done and will ever be done. Ah, Dolly, this is senseless wordy nothings. I am sorry. I have only silence.

A teaching from Sumari, an ancient sound language from another universe: We need not feel fatigue, energy is ours. When we are unbalanced we become tired. Our hands and fingers enable us to rejuvenate our bodies. We have to want to be well and not use illness as a reason for not being energized and having the intent to accomplish whatever it is we choose to do.

We are to love our moments within time. We choose them. We chop wood and carry water and we are to love the menial moment or the inspirational one as having no difference. Fatigue is an indication that dislike and imbalance has interrupted our state of health.

The universe we are creating with others has a supply of energy that is for our use.

Here is an exercise in energy:

Place the thumb of the right hand in the center of the palm of the left hand. The palm of the hand represents the sense of total harmony. This area is the director. This is the area of total energy. Press the thumb with medium pressure and hold as long as you choose. Reverse the thumb and do the same in the right palm with the left thumb with medium pressure for as long as you choose.

Hold the left thumb with the right hand. Hold it as long as you choose. You will gradually feel a pulse. Reverse and do the same with the right thumb. The thumb is the director for head discomfort, breathing, abdominal discomfort, chest and lung constriction, and reproductive organs. It helps speech and clears thinking. It helps muscle tone, aids digestion, helps with relaxation of the hips and back and with the pain of corns and calluses.

Hold the left ring finger with the right hand as long as you choose and you will feel a pulse. Reverse hands and hold the right-hand ring finger with the left hand. This affects general well-being, backaches, breath, digestion, any discomfort of the legs and eye tension. It helps with nausea, dizziness, the nervous system, creative thinking, ankle edema, and the heart, and assists with harmonizing the entire body.

Hold the middle finger of the left hand with the right hand for as long as you choose. You will feel a pulse. Reverse hands and hold the right middle finger with the left hand. This affects breathing, the lymphatic/immune center, lungs, shoulders, neck tension, mental and emotional stress, appetite balance, and a youthful, appearance. It energizes the brain/mind and gives both alertness and calmness. This finger quietly helps regenerate the entire body.

Hold the index finger of the left hand with the right hand for as long as you choose. You will feel a pulse. Reverse hands and hold the right index finger with the left hand. This brings a sense of peace, releases pelvic stress, discomforts of elimination, and helps assimilation. It releases fears, heart conditions, chest congestion, and breathing. It helps the knees and clears the voice. It balances male/female gender differences, affects thyroid and parathyroid functions, helps prevent stroke and helps clear thoughts. It releases shoulder and neck tension, hip and leg stress and is a mental and emotional center for harmony.

Hold the little finger of the left hand with the right hand for as long as you choose. You will feel a pulse. Reverse and hold the ring finger of the right hand with the left hand. This affects the sense of happiness and joy. It releases hip, knee, and foot stress, and helps heal wounds and broken bones. It helps heart function, helps with sleep disorders and clears the head, eyes, and ears. It heals tinnitus and ringing in the ears. It clears the brain, adrenal function, circulation, and eliminates fear. It prevents and helps with any stubborn, jealous, or revengeful inclinations.

This is Jim Shin Jyutsu.

Dolly: What creates energy, Muffy?

Muffy: There are entities, all us, but nonphysical aspects of us in this dream who work on making electrons, oak trees, rabbit ears, computer screens, Cocoa Puffs™, and concrete. We are all intertwined in the now, very much like the warp and woof of a tapestry. The threads are far more complicated than our brains can handle. As a flea crawling the length of one thread, you or I would not see the whole tapestry nor would we see either the weave nor the central idea, but that does not mean it is not there. That's how "rules" get imprinted in the now. All is made in every depth and dimension in every world and universe. I guess scientists call it standing waves? We are all parts of all that. Dream to be sure. But here we are, two fleas crawling our thread. There is a lot more going on besides our quiet crawling!

It would seem that we have put together a serious set of dream rules and regulations that insist on obedience from every dreamer. Sooner or later (usually we humans keep putting off reading the fine print and, thus, we opt for a passel of lifetimes) we get the rules pasted on our foreheads and wrists and we pay attention or not. The rules say balanced karma is the absolute bottom line so if we do not learn to read, we'll stay in first grade until we do learn to read!

Across the board we are required by an earthen monopoly agreement to sort out how to play the game, and its black and white duality on this level. The directive is do it! Otherwise we are in our own "doo doo" for as much time as it takes. Quite right, Dolly, that is the name of the game we are all agreeing to play. Dream it is and dream it will be until we "get it." All made up by us and when we come to play in duality, we do indeed (eventually) learn to play by the rules. For some of us, the seemingly impossible merely takes a little longer, or a lot longer.

I am not obligated to admire all problem solving. I do feel obligated to understand how an individual goes about solving problems.

━━━ ⊠⬦⊠ ━━━

Dolly: Is there a difference in intelligence and wisdom?

Muffy: Let's talk about those.

1. Intelligence is the innate ability to reason and draw conclusions that might work well to resolve conflict, further intent or, gain a goal based on previous experience that seemed successful and not digging the same hole over and over if the original idea is not gained.

2. Wisdom is to know the difference! Or, as someone once said, "A smart (intelligent) person knows what to say. A wise person knows whether or not to say it."

3. Knowing, ah, not so glib with this one. Knowing has to do with careful examining of one's beliefs, scrutinizing every single aspect of one's belief system, every tiny shred. Then and only then can one take on slowly and carefully over perhaps a lifetime, or many lifetimes, the quietly accepted knowing that allows for a serene inner peace (great grace as a gift can in rare instances supplant and/or add to hopefully graceful quiet knowing.)

In this dream universe, everything is beginning to accelerate. It may take a century. We will see the tip of what is really happening to us. On the etheric level there is a truly ongoing war zone (all dream too, of course). We are getting lots of help from other levels, otherwise this acceleration could be much harder for us. DNA will change. We are changing and it's needed so we can be aware of our fifth-dimension intent. Some will apparently make the shift with little noticed outward trauma. Almost all of the future hue and cry for endless drug prescriptions will be the attempt to cover up transformation difficulties on a physical level, not consciously of course. If there are methods for avoiding certain consequences of shifting I do not know them. We are in for a roller-coaster ride for a number of years. Interesting and not easy, yet here we are after twenty-six thousand years doing it again, and this time we will succeed. I have only one method, which is hardly helpful when your body is in pain!

Thought is only thought (Andrew Cohen). We are thinking our world into three dimensions. Even so, it is only thought, absolutely only thought, and it sounds deceptively simple. Certainly, however, the practical implications about thought are enormous. Most of us have a very difficult time thinking that thought is only thought because we so often think that thought is self. My thoughts are me. And, surely a body in pain makes it seem a whale of a lot easier to believe that thought is indeed "my personal self!"

It is so easy to believe that what we think is who we are, yet any thought we have of any kind has no self-nature whatsoever, no significance except what we choose to give it. We'd escape the trauma of acceleration into another dimension without a doubt if we stopped being distracted by our inner movement of thought and our devotion to the belief that we are real and thought is real. We could then observe from "above the battle-ground" and find a kind of overall peace and understanding.

This is the only method I know about for getting through the next time in history that affects each one of us.

We must re-examine every tiny shred of our personal belief system, tracing our beliefs to their sources and making changes in the beliefs we hold or dropping them totally and embracing new beliefs more in keeping with our intent and goals. We will then automatically change what we project outwardly into what we call our world. We will then perceive our life as having changed to match the beliefs we now proclaim we have changed for the better (hopefully). This can take time or can be instantaneous. How can we see whether we have truly changed our beliefs? By noting that changes are taking place in our lives and, again, this can be instantaneous or it can take time. But changes in our lives, when our beliefs are changed, must happen! We make our reality by the beliefs we hold. Change a belief and outward change must take place. Perception follows projection. That is the way of things on this physical level in which we find ourselves.

The dream is ours. It is not out there. It is in our mind. We project the dream outwardly and then perceive what we choose to see, depending on our beliefs about physical non-reality. Thus, if the dream is ours, and it is in agreement with others on our dream-stage, then we are in charge of what happens in our dream. The beliefs about sin, guilt, and fear usually win out and few humans truly understand that they make what they experience. They choose it and either find a way to change what they do not want in their dream, or as most humans do, they shirk the responsibility of examining their beliefs and changing what they do not like. Most humans would rather blame God or fate or genes or the guy next door.

So, my answer is: of course we are in charge. Of course we are responsible and, of course, it is our dream and we can do it the way we choose, which we are doing every second, only most do not realize that it is so (and prefer not to know). What is perceived each moment is exactly what is asked for, knowingly or not. "We are doing it!"

⊷ ⊱⊰ ⊶

Dolly: Did I start the dream millions of years ago, Muffy?

Muffy: The one starting and continuing the dream of Dolly is Dolly or whatever name you use; "a rose is still a rose." You allow yourself total freedom to do as you please in your dreams, as we all do, and we also tailor our dreams to include others who agree to be in our dreams and in their own dreams that do not necessarily include us. It's a complicated, creative, intensely focused energy that is us on many levels in infinite realities; possible, probable, and parallel, all interconnected and incredibly powerful. Yet, all is a dream. All is made up. All is good theatre and all is choosing what to project in what seems to our senses is an outward world. "Projection makes perception" (*A Course in Miracles*) and we interact within the projected world we all agree is our field of operation. And, make no mistake, we do love our individual, creative, special, unique dreams! We do love our way of believing. We do love our capability as playwrights and we do believe we are who we think we are. In fact, we insist on just that and we fight and do battle at the slightest suggestion that all is a dream. All is made up and all is not as it seems.

⊷ ⊨✦⊨ ⊷

Dolly: What is happening in Heaven, Muffy?

Muffy: The only happening is that God created us as one. Now that is a happening! You do not exist; neither do I nor does anyone else in dreams. We are dream figures and we choose to believe we are real. We are not real as we think of ourselves. We are real in Heaven, as one where we never left and never could. All else is made up by you and me and everyone else, as actors on a stage of our own making. We choose to be so intensely focused in our dreams that we refuse to even entertain the possible thought that we are not real. What is left after ego is quietly replaced by the real self? That is the eternal bliss, the changeless being of reality. It is a tough road to travel and worth it, but it is as rocky as can be. That is why the projected world continues in seeming existence and has for eons. And, as I have said before, it will not cease to be by Saturday night.

The only way out is to forgive one's self and others for the mazes we make and to laugh at our "amazing" ways. Then perhaps having forgiven self and all others, we can begin again in a dream that never happened and never could. Yet, here we are so we just laugh and smile and shovel and dig and smile some more and get on with it.

Yes, it seems you are still here (you are still talking to me so I assume you are still here) and correct. Apparently you are here for whatever time you choose. I think perhaps it is safe to say you are not going to find yourself home in Heaven where you never left by dinnertime! For not realizing that we can laugh and admit that we have not got a clue about how to get things as we would wish, that wishing is a child's avenue, that changing our beliefs about the world will change our world, that we are safely in Heaven where that happens in life though few of us admit to it, that God loves us as he created us and all sadness and sorrow and lack and "I wants" and all the misery and, yes, the joys of this position we assume on planet earth, all is of our own doing, in agreement with others.

Our lives are of our own making. We must examine our beliefs and discard those that do nothing to help us on our journey. We must retain those beliefs that serve us well and embrace new ones that enable us to trot on. By trotting on, we can, by noticing and being aware, see and hear and understand how we are doing sometimes with lots of understanding and sometimes very little. And it has to be okay. Why does it have to be okay? Because we are on a journey and that is the exact place we are until we are not. We learn as we go.

I think of life as a way of seeing, a way of becoming, a way of learning and a way of changing. I see life here in three dimensions as a way of teaching self that we are here by choice. That is our dream that we can see and laugh at our dream-selves struggling, and at one and the same time know we are safely at home in Heaven and that this is all made up as in a stage play.

That attitude allows for jokes and laughter and some "Mona Lisa smiles" aimed at the self as we work our way from birth to dropping our pajamas and opting for other fields of becoming in other dreams of our own making or realizing that all is a dream and laugh quietly at the absurdity that this earthly life is of such importance! It is not. It is one more dream of our infinite numbers of self-made dreams. Once that is accepted, it becomes a game, earth Monopoly® if you like, to learn the rules and choose a life-dream that has integrity as exactly what it is, a dream. And, to get on with the job of completing the dream in a way that should we look back, we can at the very least say, "Ah, not too shabby."

Every person here believes in magic. Yes, the very life dream we are living is a journey into magic. Yes, one's life is laid out for others to see. We cannot help that. We teach every second who we are. By living our dream each moment we are showing any person or other being exactly who we are in that moment. Should another care to look or even choose to do more than merely look, we are who we are and that person in this dream is on stage each moment showing anyone who cares to find out exactly who we are by our behavior. Thus, every human on planet earth each moment is teaching. Do not get strangled from the neck up. Just accept you are dreaming. You do not like all the aspects of your dream. Set about changing a few beliefs at a time and know that you are loved by many and that you are safe in Heaven where you never left. Then get on with sorting out how you want to spend your moments on this dream stage. Then you just do that.

——— ⊷✠⊷ ———

Dolly: Because I am still sleeping?

Muffy: Dear one, we are all asleep to some degree. If we were not, we would not be in this dimension. We would either have realized it is a dream and elected to not dream on or we would have elected to do something else. We make our reality. It is up to us to choose each moment in what we call "the tool of time" and to choose with as much discernment as we can muster, not berate ourselves for what we call failure, and to get on with life. We seem to agree we are here, no matter how many times we might be told we are dreaming. We do not believe that for an instant. We think this is real, real, real and it is! It's a real dream! Are you laughing? Please do. Be silly about it and just play your Dolly part on stage to the best of your acting ability. Yes, I am smiling. Sort out your dream and get on with it. I am sure you are doing just fine. Allow for whatever appears in your dream on stage. Do what in the moment you can do to smile more and as I say constantly, just trot on.

That is the internal dialogue. "I know this is magic that I am using in a dream of my own making." Quality of life is in your hands to determine. You have to assume you know the best answer and then you make happen what you know is best. Things do happen for a reason. Yes, things that seem to occur outside of self are mirrors of our inner lives. It is true.

Every tiny aspect of what seems to be the world "out there" are parts of our own inner selves that mirror who we are and how we are working on various parts of our lives we choose to live here in three-dimensions. Most of us pretend that is not so. We often prefer not to give that a thought. The world is out there "doing it to us." We are victims. That is the general acceptance of the world we live in. That is, however, an erroneous belief.

What we experience is what we make each and every moment in every life in a kind of unending now. We are the ones who must sort out our moments and learn what we are telling ourselves. The lessons we are giving to ourselves are all before our faces if we but look. Most of us would rather not look, "thank you very much."

Every tiny second of who Muffy is as she jumps out of her stall each morning to face the script she is writing in her own play which is her life. You were never promised a rose garden. Yes, always to be seeking the "what is it for" as your moments unroll and to see your life-moments in the way of the cat. Perhaps it is your script, your life and your questions. You alone know the answers for your life.

——— ≕✦≕ ———

Dolly: What about healing, Muffy?

Muffy: There is no such thing as "healings sent." There is no sending anything, anywhere. There is no anywhere. There is no going nor coming nor is there other than this. Life seems to be here and real. We believe it is so and all the king's horses and all the king's men would not persuade us differently! However, our senses lie to us and though they work fine for this three dimensional level, things are not as they seem, try as we might to make that truth not true. Life here is a choice. We each in turn make the choice to make a life in this dimension. It is a dream. It is what we give to ourselves as a kind of stage play with props and curtains and a stage and actors and an audience all scripted by us.

What is it for, you ask? To teach ourselves lessons we think we need. To work out the ways of becoming more than we believe we are in the moment. Each life lived, all now, are lessons we as the creative playwrights determine are ways for us to grasp, embrace, and teach ourselves more about who we are. The goal, you ask? To maintain our individuality, our unique personality, our conviction that we are real and our lives are important. Guess what? Our lives feel and seem important to us, the individual, and they are important to the dreamer who is us. In the big picture? Not really. The real honest truth is that we are all one Son/Child of God and perfect in Heaven where we never left.

Meanwhile, back at the family farm in New Hampshire, someone in her script for today must feed the cat, wash dishes, look for a job, face crooked-legged ponies and weepy-eyed ones too and think about winter coming, hay and bedding and, well, you know, all the myriad moments that every human in its own way must face each "day of the dream." So what is the obligation in those moments we believe are real?

It is to live life with integrity, honesty, as joyously as possible and with a smile. No whimpering, no victim-hood attitude, no anything except the willingness to do all we can to make our personal world a better way to be and to then offer a helping hand to anyone who seems out there in their own dream.

That is the answer to "what is it for?" To be able to look back if we choose and see a life lived that is not shabby and that is lived with a certain "It's okay to be me" and a life lived with a sense of "I did it and gave it my best shot!" A life lived not to weep and tremble and be fearful and feel guilty because the life we make seems not perfect.

Of course it is not perfect and this life often seems senseless! And, in so many ways, it is senseless! Yet here we are so we make the best of it. Do we have to live it? Yes, it seems we do until we do not. Do we have to like it? No, we do not, in spite of protestations to the contrary. As long as we seem to still be here, it is pretty obvious we do love it even with all the seeming "downers" we make for ourselves. We move on as we uncover the lessons we give ourselves. We "move on" as we garner strength to tackle yet another lesson. We "move on" as we discover that as one lesson seems learned, there are twelve more in its place. There is a never-ending line of lessons we offer to ourselves at center stage and we must deliver.

I do think, however, and do believe that when a tiny flicker of a moment occurs wherein a truth wings its way to the surface of our minds and we grab that winged bit, it is a sacred blink of knowing. A tiniest drop of what Heaven is like and, therefore, I called that little dewdrop dear and blessed. It is the blink of time and space and all things gone. In their place is joy, unbound by things. So my sentence remains a truth for me as

Dream 021185136851
Dolly

I see it. I agree it's barely a fraction of time standing still. Even so, it's what I call "lesson learned."

—————— ⚍ ——————

Dolly: Why do people get sick going to other countries on long airplane rides other than the obvious germ issue?

Muffy: Germs are merely the "outward aspect" of something on which to hang one's hat and talk about. There are no germs, though we can certainly find some by looking. Do not forget the scientists' findings that waves and particles are there when we choose to make them there if indeed we need to blame someone or something such as a germ or a virus.

—————— ⚍ ——————

Dolly: Is there no reason to feel guilty when one harms another?

Muffy: Guilt is guilt. Guilt for most minds is the belief that one is not perfect. Yes, strange places, feelings of inadequacy, guilt for not being perfect, for not knowing everything, for not finding things as one can wish or hope for. It's not home. It's not what I prefer. It's not what I want. Then that word, guilt, leaps up and says: "Oh you guilty person for complaining, for being tired, for not being Mr. Wonderful except outwardly. Oh you guilty person for feeling as you do! Oh you guilty person for being you!" And, we take out our feelings on our bodies. We call it germs or bugs, but it's not. It is the wrong-slanted mind saying: "You are guilty for not being what you ought to be, so get sick by having caught a snappy and on-alert buglet to blame!" Having capably projected one's anger and frustration on one's stomach or whatever is the usual way we solve our problems. Humans do that. It's the ego world at its creative best. That is what the world is, projection.

⊷ ⋻✛⋻ ⊷

Dolly: And what about pain?

Muffy: Pain is always projected outwardly when we cannot seem to bear it. Whether it's the stomach or the neighbors or the boss or the dog, projections seem only to place blame away from us. One's stomach or one's shoulder or back or left foot all give a respite at least for a time from facing the "guilt of being" that we all carry about as loose luggage. So there we are, projection. It is how humans solve their problems and the world keeps spinning the ego. We found a way. Are we not too, too clever?

To look at all this and forgive it means: "Ah me. I am dreaming and dreaming is fun and at times not so fun but daydreaming it is and I hold myself not guilty of anything other than dreaming. I blame no one, including myself for our dreams.

Such ephemeral stuff is not the stuff of guilt and stomach bugs. I am innocent as is everyone else in my dream. There is no blame. Nothing happened. It is all a dream!" I admit it does take some doing to arrive at the firm conviction that all is a dream and nothing ever really happened.

And I admit at the physical level that irritated stomachs and all the ravages we project on our bodies and into what we believe is an "out there" world and does not necessarily change "in the twinkling of an eye." Maybe the land of make-believe, which we call "the world," will not seem to change at all. Physical reality is not entirely predictable. Inwardly? Ah yes, the landscape changed inwardly. No more guilt about anything! One simply allows the dream, whatever its makeup. We accept responsibility for our dream. We smile at our silly ways and peace reigns for the most part until our dream ends. Not everyone is ready to do the above in this moment. However, that is the goal for everyone. And, sooner or later, everyone will accept the need to laugh at our human ego-laden determinations to have a world exactly as we perceive it, out there and "doing it to us." We will awaken and realize we have dreamed and dreamed and dreamed and we will laugh aloud.

Dolly: What is the difference in our physical body and our energy nature?

Muffy: Our energy body is what tells the brain to heal the body and make things happen physically. Every person who heals does so from etheric energy to physical energy. I can see the process and wonder if I can put it in words. I never have before as it is not my field of interest. I think I can though. I might try.

Dolly: And do people even choose to be ill?

Muffy: Dear one, illness is a choice. Yes, it is always a choice. Fear and guilt create illness. Of course, anything chosen as a help, aspirin or whatever, needs to be offered, but overall, illness is a choice. If the aspirin magic works and illness is allayed, then the choice of illness was changed. If all the magic in the world does not do a darned thing, then you know the choice is illness continued until it isn't.

The majority of humans in our world are fearful; fearful of life, of death, of taxes, of one another, of the future, of the past. Many carry the baggage of religious upbringings and a major fear of God the Creator. And why not? A God made in the image of us? Good Heavens, that brand of God is somebody to be feared and that is for sure! A God who in the end gets those who fear him by knocking them over dead. And the fear and guilt of a lifetime, lifetimes known or unknown, build on the slim hope that maybe God's Son's death will make up for the sins and guilt and fear. What a round robin of deplorable beliefs and endless scourging and dismay. Then there are those who have no fears of a creator, because we do not believe in the possibility of a God made in the image of us. Thus, we leave the door at least part way open to understanding and a lessening of the mystery of what this is all for.

Most humans live and die never knowing nor caring that this is an illusion/dream and made-up theatre. True enough, the majority of humans simply live, enjoy, suffer, and leave the planet to return and do it over. Whether they remember or not matters little. However, to those who give time and effort to thinking through the possibility of this being a dream, as Shakespeare told us, and we the actors and the bit players, "the stage is the thing." What it does for those who care is the letting go of fear, not denial. There is no fear. There cannot be! A loving creator is where we live and have our being. If all is illusion and we are safely in heaven where we never left in an unchanging, unchanged, eternally blissful state, then accepting, believing, understanding, and knowing that this is but a stage play means quite simply that we are free. Free to live in all our fantasy lives and focus where we will, knowing we are doing it and knowing that we are the central character of our own script. And knowing full well that when we are ready, we can cease dreaming and be home. Knowing this is theatre we are making means we are allowing for what we are choosing, laughing over our impossible choice and making that impossible choice as elegant and grace-filled as we can.

＊＋≡＋＋

Fear and guilt and death are not partners and the pathway to heaven was never constructed. It was never needed. We are already there.

＊＋≡＋＋

We can give intellectual assent until all hell freezes over to the fact that it is a dream and illusion, but make no mistake, we are so deeply focused here we well do believe this is real! In so believing, we must not deny that fears of mowers may need help, that daisies grow and make the neighbors want to choke you, that making hay is sweaty, gut-wrenching work that gives our muscles a test of fitness. We must not deny all that and face that sometimes this level is a puissant non-working nightmare. The fact that you can laugh at your dreams is the key.

It seems to be what we do, inflict physical form with our mental notions of guilt and fear. The ultimate answer is to allow, understand, accept, and await getting better or not. That is the answer primarily for those totally, absolutely, and unequivocally devoted to enlightenment here and now. Most have not that kind of willing and humble absolute resolution. A way to undo feelings of guilt and fear may not be a logical way at all. That is intuitive. If we truly love ourselves, truly believe we are worthy, then that love of self would heal bodies and allow for deep inner understanding of what is. Most are on that path. Most, I daresay, are not as yet arrived.

<hr/>

Dolly: So healing any illness requires only forgiveness?

Muffy: Oh, you are funny, Dolly! Forgiveness is understanding that nothing ever happened and that dreams of any kind are dreams and illusions and then we laugh, laugh, and laugh at ourselves for thinking otherwise!

So someone returned cancer-free, and having experienced a classroom unlike most, and are they awake now? Do they wake up and know they dream? Are you aware of what you gave yourself? A great gift of recognition as to what is life and what is not life? Are you seeing that you gave this magical journey to yourself as a way to teach you to truly see? Well, and do you see?

All ignorance in time is erased and replaced by knowing and certainly every human will not be all done with ignorance by this Memorial Day!

I do not think that sheep, those who are willing to follow unthinkingly where the herd is headed, are so much dishonest as they are unthinking. Thinking and determining for oneself takes energy and time and consideration. Many are unwilling, maybe even unable in some lives to do more than follow.

That is not dishonesty; it's ignorance. But more than that, it is a matter of not being ready. The time is not right for some humans who could be called "sheep" to take their lives seriously enough to ponder, peruse, consider, and form their own determinations based on the best information they can muster. It is not so much dishonest; it is quite simply easier to follow. To be sure, when one does know the difference, one is responsible.

To stay centered and awake:

Wherever you are, no matter what you are doing, thinking seeing, dreaming, screaming, nodding, smiling:

1. Feel yourself in your body.

2. Do you feel you in your limbs, face, and legs?

3. Are you aware of you in your earth suite in your body?

4. That is awareness of being.

5. Now maintain that each moment for the rest of this lifetime. That is enlightenment.

Dolly: Has life here been that much more difficult than on Tara?

Muffy: Ah, well, we are Lyran and Orion and, of course, Zeta Reticuli and Lyrans are the forefathers of Pleiadians. We are all hybrids. Some less so than others and no matter what color and type, we trot on.

Yes, we Pleiadians rarely get angry; we are kinder than many, we serve others, and we support and affirm what is in front of us. We walk the second and third mile with anyone who needs us. We are, for the most part, not anxious to be noticed. We are shy and prefer to be unknown. We do what is before us and we do it because it is there to do. Yes, most of us are extremely loving, often passionately so.

We understand and appreciate animals. Indeed, on Erra, animals and people communicate openly. We love trees (some of us adore dandelions and daisies), we laugh a lot and we send tea bags in the mail. We find silly little things to brighten someone's day and everyone I know loves children if they are convinced that this level is illusion. But there are dark forces, the reptilian-related humans. We prefer to leave them to their own destruction.

Dolly: Why take on duality, Muffy?

Muffy: Harder, true enough. Sometimes I despair of the latest snake in my path.

On the other hand, all is perfect. We have never been other than perfect. We could not be other than perfect. We are in Heaven and created perfect as God's son or daughter, a seamless garment where God and God's creation are one, though we are not God. We are the created one. Perfection cannot have an opposite. Thus, anything that could be considered opposite or different, etc., is not real. The only reality is God in Heaven, and we are there.

Now, if we are perfect and in Heaven, then we have no need to incarnate and strive for perfection, i.e. sainthood. We incarnate to be individual, personal, and unique. We love being who we are, a focused personality. We are willing to endure all manner of inconvenience so long as we can maintain our "Dolly" and our "Muffy" identity. We incarnate to show God that we can be "me."

So we are born and we die and we make new identities and focus on being self. There is no time and so all is now, sort of like pancakes one on top of the other. A kind of TV special if you will: "pick a particular chess game and play out a life."

Yes, given enough time, and it seems we are mightily slow at this, we gradually gain a bit of insight as to whether it is better not to beat our neighbor over the head with a nearby rock and drag his wife and daughter to our cave in the other valley. Yes, gradually over time, I suppose billions of years, we get the idea that perhaps there is a way that does not include bloodletting. (We have not gotten that lesson completely learned, but I do think we may well be in the sight of the idea of dropping the dagger.)

So, yes, in the dream we do appear to be at the beginning of getting things sorted out and put to rights. Higher states are one way to describe it. I would be inclined to say that we gain insight as to how we can aim toward excellence. Even the idea of excellence and what it means is a drawn-out process that will not have been completed by bath time next Saturday evening. So, to accomplish and actually live lives of excellence it seems to me is admirable and in and of itself. Yes, it is still a dream-state and subject to the inevitable. Dreams go their way and only reality remains. To the best of my understanding that is so.

A dog that lives with a human with insight, sensitivity and joy will show forth those qualities. However, it is my opinion that the dog already has those qualities in abundance! It is the dog that shows the human how to bring out the qualities of playfulness and honesty and loyalty. Pets show people who they are. As for what are called wild animals (they dislike being called animals and much prefer a proper term such as other being), I believe that most of them are fearful for their lives and that tells us how unskilled people are in their abilities to be kind and loving and caring of others.

They do well to maintain a safe distance from people. Their wildness is a safety factor for living on earth. And, of course, the earth way of eat or be eaten comes into the equation. Many of the creatures now here are hybrids of their original species. They agree to be here to enable humans to live here and grow. In my opinion, no one would be able to live more than ten or fifteen years if felines and canines and equines did not agree to be here too. People need their energy so the animals agree to be here. They show great courage and caring to do so. Animals are brilliant in their own way. Each species, ants and earthworms and felines and elephants, and of course dolphins, penguins and so on, are brilliant. Only people do not see them in their wholeness. Humans are still blind. Animals are so different in their entirety than people are aware.

⤝⤞✠⤝⤞

   Harsh night
   Storm cloud banners
   The skies unroll
   Doubt and dread assail my fainting soul.
   Clamor! Harsh bells. They hammer the toll
   Pray reach the intended goal
   Dim to me. Cruel wind does blow
   Oh God please help. He does not know.
   At dawn
   Morning lights the days

And the sleeping mountains glow
Lies a certain moon-lit splendor
In the valley there below.
Sleeping in their woodland ways
Awakening to morning's first displays,
The birds come singing and winds do blow
Small seeds of blessings to and fro
No secret loss the earth declares
My heart is light, no pain nor cares.
Leaving there the trailing night
They vanished with the dawning light.
Trotting the well-worn path I go
See now the straying summer rose
Leaves dancing in the morning air,
I tell myself in love and prayer.
He knows, He knows.

Dolly: What is sin, Muffy?

Muffy: The willingness to take on duality and become able to forgive ourselves for making life so hard, for not accepting that this is all dream, we are making it, for not realizing that we can laugh and admit that we have not got a clue about how to get things as we would wish, that wishing is a child's avenue, that changing our beliefs about the world will change our world, that we are safely in Heaven where we never left, that we feel guilty and fearful of much that happens in life though few of us admit to it, that God loves us as he created us and all sadness and sorrow and lack of "I wants" and all the misery and, yes, the joys of this position we assume on planet earth, all is of our own doing in agreement with others.

Our lives are of our own making. We must examine our beliefs and discard those that do nothing to help us on our journey. We must retain those beliefs that serve us well and embrace new ones that enable us to trot on. We cannot attempt a perfect detachment from illusion. I think that would mean total ego-less-ness, perhaps a few actual humans can live here in egoless duality but not for long. It is just too damned hard to do! One can do it when grace allows (I call it grace and think I know what grace is but I rarely talk about it). Anyway, what we learn is that detachment is not needed. It is the realization that illusion is illusion, not real, and then we can laugh and laugh and get on with illusion until we decide to leave it "behind." We bring truth to illusion and illusion vanishes because it is seen for what it is, nothing.

We have lots of less than perfect moments in our dreams. We often choose unwisely and make mistakes in discernment. We gradually learn to make choices that suit us better than previous poor choices, or so we think, if indeed we are bent in the direction of choosing a better way. (Many are not bent in that direction, of course.) We make our way in duality, certainly missing the mark, meaning ignorance, lack, or poor choices, either deliberate or not. We can acknowledge our follies, smile, and dig in again if we choose. It is up to us.

However, sin is just a word, a biblical one pretty much, and most often brings on the image of the vengeful personality of a God that must punish transgressors. This is kindergarten stuff! We must needs have at least gotten a few gold stars prior to getting into the first grade and then trotting on minus the vengeful father image and into the concept that God neither knows nor cares about our dreaming self who has forgotten where we really live and have our being.

It must be so that our souls remain unsullied and untouched by human foibles. It's ego that digs ditches for us to fall into and ego that chops logs to cross our paths. It is ego that wants what it wants, preferably last week but certainly right now! All souls must then live sweetly, not snarled in the dreams laid upon hearts and souls and then dwell not in nothingness. It then follows that it is the mind that chooses a less than better way and causes itself to feel downhearted and dis-spirited. Our dream-lives lead us not toward home but far afield. The daisies here distract us, yet surely beneath their golden faces is truth? Are we not made in and for an eternity where a flower, like a soul, lives fresh and lively always?

Dolly: So to a large extent, it does not matter whether it is a dream or not. There are "rules of the game" so to speak?

Muffy: Amen, and how! And you better believe it; people are fiercely attuned to vengeance and restitution for every tiny speck.

Well, Dolly, it is dream indeed; however, on levels other than this one, and even at times on this one, justice is indeed insisted upon. Most do try here but often badly. Agreed? For example, in Summerland, where the more complete view of what is and what is not, what is clear (it is not possible to lie in Summerland), teachers and mentors take a "previous life" apart thread by thread with the consciousness who has "returned" for review.

One's entity, the orange, holding all the map-pin personalities, does not agree that murder and mayhem are to be ignored and that rape and pillage are just fine as it is "only a dream." Even in a dream, which most humans do not think is a dream, most people consider duality as a reality, real, seriously real. And, there is agreement that justice will be paid by incarnates, very much so.

All must learn how to comfort themselves in a dreamscape, which most everyone you meet believes real. There is very much wrong in dreams. There are codes of agreement and on all dream levels, justice and balance will be insisted upon to the last farthing. It will be a very long time before humans agree that all is a dream, and even if everyone by some odd change of belief truly agreed that all is a dream, even so, a standard, a code, a set of rules would continue to be very much incorporated into the dream. All have a mass belief about penitence, restitution, eye for an eye. There are courts in duality, but are they always perfect? Good Lord, no, but it is an agreement that there is a justice system. Well, that system, taken to other heights, is also part of the dream, and the dream is us, very determined that those who transgress pay for their transgressions by making restitution.

Hitler will spend many lives in severe learning situations until he gets it. It is not allowed to point a finger and say "you die" without having a heavy toll of restitution laid upon that very consciousness. Also remember that Hitler, as a symbol, was the carrier of each one of every human's hatred and malicious intent toward one another. He agreed to be that symbol and he was that. What a role to play! His life and the lives of any and all who are not on the path of re-remembering who we truly are, and can we not say that in certain moments every one of us forgets to remember?

So in some ways we are a part of Hitler's anger and fury and vicious attitude, just as we are involved with every single malicious moment of hatred ever perpetuated on anyone who seems outside of self in all of our world's history and, no doubt, other world's history as well! Even if it is all a dream, and it is, even so we learn by experience and Hitler has much to learn. Then again, so does each one of us, each in our own way.

When we do not live the best we know, then we are mistaken, ignorant, lazy and uncaring. Who can say if we are truthful and that we have not ever lived those negative qualities at some moment or in many moments? Yet history drones on. The dream rolls on. Ah, the tardy ways in which only a small percent of humanity is barely beyond the level of integrity. It is going to take a while before we get it. Agreed? Yet, one day time will be no more and each in turn will have figured the score and paid their bill and moved on. A lengthy and tiresome, dirty business. It is not pretty, not encouraging, not pleasant mostly with ego having its day on the stage of what we call life. Restitution is ever a requirement of each of us in turn. We choose justice when we finally realize there is no other way.

There is no order of ineptitude, no order of idiocy, no order of ignorance, and no order of anything with a ladder of this is better and this is worse. Thinking we are living reality is horror enough without figuring ways to find Hitler worse than deliberately pulling wings off flies. On the surface, it seems worse to rape a six year old or genocide. That is our senses at work in illusion. In the bigger picture, it is all lumped as insanity and we are insane. That is for sure.

＋•＋ ▆✦▆ ＋•＋

Now, on a practical level, good old boy Hitler has reparation to do big time. The scales of justice do prevail. I think he has rein-

carnated as a lowly nun in the streets of Calcutta, there to work out his days and lives learning about humility and patience and greed and all the rest. His litany of horrors will be carefully and exquisitely meted out to him in every way. Restitution is ever a requirement of each of us in turn. We choose justice when we finally realize there is no other way. That choosing remains in the world of illusion, however, and has nothing to do with the fact that Hitler and Jack the Ripper are in Heaven as one. Hitler's personality is undergoing review and returns, and you can well believe, to every last farthing and are as deeply inflicted by himself as any he perpetuated on others. That is the absolute scale of justice. That is personality, illusion, hallucination, duality, dream and he is paying his dues and more. Reality is his life in Heaven has not changed and never will. It never could but in Heaven, his illusionary name, Hitler, is unknown and unknowable. There is no sign. There is ignorance aplenty, horror, insanity, foolishness, and mistakes but our oneness is untouched by such. God neither knows nor cares about our dreams. They do not exist. They are not Heaven. They are not perfection. They are not real.

Dolly: And what if people continue to ignore the place this dream is taking us?

Muffy: There is no such thing as sin. It is a word that we have come to equate with bad deportment in the physical, non-reality dream-scale and something God would be miserable knowing about and would have to do the fatherly thing and bring out the switch or the belt. Well, God knows nothing whatever of such goings on, nor could be a part of such. It is not perfection.

Remember that Jesus is a very elevated consciousness from a distant galaxy and dimension all within. I am not talking space and light years. I am talking inner distance from our three-dimensional space. There is no outside world. We project our thoughts outwardly and they look like a space world. It is not real. Think of a circle. We are here in three dimensions and are the outward line of the circle and then spiral inwardly from the line of the circle. Jesus' galaxy is very much on an inward spiral. He is not God. He is a form just as we are but his form is more like a cloud of light than density. Like our physical bodies, he is able to bi-locate so he can be whatever is needed in an outward form to plant his information in any reality he chooses.

If he was observed in India as being real, and he was, he was more Indian looking and if in South America, more of that type. He was indeed born and raised as the Bible states, a Jew, and his travels were the traders' routes teaching and offering his human self first. Then, if he could, adding some "seeds of information and understanding" about more than just finding water and food and survival. He never forgot who he is. He never fell asleep and dreamed as we dream. He remembers. He is one of several great teachers who have appeared among us to remind us of who we are and where we really dwell; Buddha, Moses, etc. Jesus plans a return (really his name is Jeshua in more formal terms; Jesua when he is talking with friends).

When in his teaching guise, along the trade routes, he was Jewish in appearance with dark, thick, somewhat curly hair and darkish skin. He was perhaps five feet nine inches with a slender build. He had beautiful dark eyes, a Jewish face with high cheekbones and a somewhat aquiline nose. He had deep-set, large eyes, a tall forehead and a strong face. Most of all, he had a deeply caring demeanor and was very, very kind. He will appear before you so clearly that you could have stood up and hugged him, though you will not. You will look at one another and remember our relationship as time friends, time friends of endless ages. You will remember clearly, as Qua told you years earlier. He wants you to remember and to not forget. (Please understand that these are mere words. It is all we have and they fall far short of what actually takes place.) And, then he will say to you, "Shall we begin." Then he will leave. That may sound sad and it may sound too brief and it may sound preposterous but make no mistake, you will never forget. He will always remain clear to you and you will feel no sadness nor other than how lovely to have had such an experience. That will linger and remain ever there. It is a great gift you will receive.

And, if you ask what he meant, well, he means to teach which is what you did starting at age fourteen. His visit will be to assure you that more is to come. This is not a big deal. It is all part of what each one of us chooses to do with our lives. Yours is this. Each person teaches in an individual way. We teach what we are. We cannot do otherwise. He is a very handsome man. He will remind you a lot of your mom's side of the family, the girls actually. Yes, your mama's family were very much Hebrew in other lives.

Honesty and integrity are rare and valuable attributes in this world. Only the honest have a chance of escaping the traps of their own making. Egomaniacs and sheep alike are being dishonest with themselves. Certainly the qualities of honesty and integrity are vitally important qualities. As there is no world, those qualities do not apply to a world that does not exist. They are simply qualities of neither rare nor not rare. They are qualities of spirit and those qualities, if recognized and if embraced by a human, certainly do contribute to a not too shabby stage performance in our dream-illusion.

Honesty is certainly a quality to embrace. As for "escaping the traps," if a human is honest then it would follow that those "traps" become learning lessons in duality and not traps at all. Each moment in our life here is programmed and meant to teach us what we decide we want to learn. If we do not pay attention, then the lesson, or trap as you call it, will return and return to our attention until we do see and learn in life after life if need be. So you see, there is no escape nor anyplace to hide. We make our reality. We set our stage. We play our parts. We learn sooner or later in time terms. We do learn! That is the intent, whether in this life or in any other. We do finally get it.

———— ⚔ ————

Egos can certainly be maniacs. Each of us in turn can attest to being at times an egomaniac, relentlessly determined to have its way ceaselessly paving its path by cunning manipulation, deceit, or dishonestly. You name it. We all can say *mea culpa* at some point to that lack of seeing ourselves in operation. To say that each human understands the extent and the meaning of the ego's demands and its determined attitude is not always true. Introspection, consideration, and intent are the inner questing for answers we each in turn must ask ourselves as our moments tick by.

To know, to learn, to see and to continue to be ego-laden and not care or give a damn is certainly dishonesty. To be ego-laden and not know is to simply not know and is ignorance and cannot be labeled dishonest. It can only be labeled dishonesty and is indeed a grave mistake and will, at some point in some life, be taken into account when that moment arrives. Oh yes, credit, or the lack thereof, is certainly due.

Humility is a word that is used badly. It does not mean one must show abject, head down, lack of worth or ability. It is a kind of badge of, "Gee everyone. Do see that I am the littlest of the little, the non-bravest of the non-brave, the lesser of the less, etc." That is arrogance in full bloom. It is saying "Gee look at me. I am so nothing. I am a shining star of nothing. I am far more nothing than you could ever be nothing."

To be humble is what we are, in essence. We are created by the most high God of all perfection and being. We did not create ourselves. We were created out of love and that love finds us. It is one creation, as one delightful to it is being if delight is an aspect of the creator. To be created out of love offers the perfect understanding of what is to be appreciative. Being humble, to have humility, is to know that we are created and beloved. I also believe it that is possible with an almighty creator that God is humbly appreciative that God is God.

───── ❈ ─────

Who are you?

You will be godmother to many, ponies and children alike. You will dream of changing diapers and cleaning stalls. You are precious. I did dream that you would be a credit to those who brought you here. I dreamed that you have your reasons, though not the coal mines any more for child or pony. There are other plans for you. No words are needed. Both pony and child communicate with silence. You understand warmth and affection and love. Don't be sad. You cannot hurt. You can only love. We two, pony and child, are the children of many mothers and what you know is love and goodness and innocence. You will share that in eternity. When one offers service and assistance to another being, one does not choose a measuring stick. One simply offers and moves on determining how well one is or is not doing and is not the reason for offering. One offers and walks away. You have no way to judge the degree of success you are having because success is not measured in any tangible way at all. It is best to offer your gift of self and let it go from your mind totally. Yes, it is really that simple.

I share what I know but I am certain it is scanty compared to what others might know about our past. My emphasis was reporting to and being involved with the galactic council.

◆━═◆═━◆

The message is humans better spend the next fifty years living from their heart charkas and understand how to increase our DNA strands so they can manage the transition from 2012 to 2017. Some will be voyagers and sail on through. Others will not be able to do that and will die and incarnate on Erra having spent some time in Summerland getting duckies in a row!

Others will not go because those who prefer to think of humans for their own ends are using holographic inserts to gain the sheep they want for their purposes, which is not to human benefit for sure. Well, many have had three hundred thousand years and nearly endless incarnations hopefully to see if they will stay in the third dimension and be exactly where they want to be.

The galactic founding nations have certainly offered and offered and offered lovingly. Humanity is in for a Nantucket sleigh ride! The next fifty years are a ticket that has not been of this might ever. Stay awake and aware. You may often actually feel the pulses of the planet with a lot going on.

———— ✠ ————

All are here in this life, illusion or dream, whatever label you choose and the first obligation is to play the earth game of Monopoly® rules. After childhood is over, one is responsible for one's meals and roof and sweaters. One pays the rent, hovel or castle, and one looks after oneself.

Enlightenment takes place when one lets go of one's ego and sees life here as a choice. One is enlightened when one lives in the moment and uses time as a way of showing forth what Jesus or the Buddha or Mohammed meant of a life of caring and offering and always with a smile.

Impersonal love means love that has no biases, no axes to grind, no needs, no grievances, no anything other than this absolute in words that are my best attempt. Love (God or Heaven) asks nothing. God is a God of love, pure love, asking nothing of us and giving us his own life. It is reciprocal. All are God's love and all mirror the perfection of God that is impersonal love. These are the best words I can find to say, impersonal love is a pure gift.

And, remember, people honestly do not know in this illusion that they are perpetrating what love really is. Individuals as egos seem forever to be loving perhaps but there seems to be a quid pro quo in it. Now maybe when they hug a tiny infant or a new puppy, they offer self in a selfless manner seeking nothing in return. They do indeed image what God's love is "in a mirror darkly." A quote? Maybe. I am unsure that to put a good word in for humans at times, let's say that when they offer self, asking nothing in return, that is close to what impersonal love is. When they offer a cute, hairy, wee laddie to a child who smiles and gleefully hugs that hairy little chap, that is love.

Maybe non-impersonal love is the smile one has on one's face as he or she enjoys the child's reaction to an offering? If that is so, then even such a generous and caring offering as a pony to a child is not nearly so impersonal as one could wish because individuals are enjoying that kid's joy, expecting that kid's joy and anticipating that kid's joy which all then share. Enjoyment is not the way God experiences creation. For want of a better term, let's say that God enjoys, loves creation, all of the universe in the same manner that is devoid of ego. That is my best attempt to describe impersonal love. Abstract love, as I see it, means the same thing, devoid of ego, asking nothing, receiving all and returning the gift of all.

Yes, it is a long, drawn out affair in time terms, usually lifetimes of learning as I understand lifetimes, which are all in this nano-second. Would you agree this is pretty intense stuff? Yes, mostly fascinating because we pull the shroud of ego so closely around our bare shoulders that we are unable to look up and see that it really is a shroud around our shoulders instead of the light of who we really are. They become more intense and understood as such, not easy but the understanding is the joy.

You are what you put forth and you are able to judge each second just how much of what you put forth is what leads to enlightenment. Enlightenment is merely a lack of baggage and baggage can be dropped in every round file every day for the rest of this dream.

Dolly will be given, given by grace, the gift of inner dancing joy. A time of inward sight, just as Qua had foretold thirty years before (plus four months). Dolly will be age thirty, January 8, 1961, at 10:42 a.m. It will bring intense awareness: Lilliput returned. You will cry out, "Lord God Heavenly King you are real! You are the one!"

Then peace beyond all understanding: star shine above and below. Four million earth years of knowing, bathed in a loving presence that leaves no place where you began and time leaves off. Suffused in light, you will lose who you are and become that light. All will be silent. All will be sublime. All in no time, no space, no thing, no form, no shape, no other. All will be as it could and must be and beyond any description whatever.

After what seems to be millions of time moments, you will come back to yourself at last. And, as at age nine, you know the real you again and will know that the accepted earth as most experience lives here is but paper maché. You treat moments shadow boxing here in what is called life in bodies on planet earth.

For thirty-eight and one half years following that experience, lessons will come on what is not love and how to reach for what is love. Nothing more and certainly nothing less. All else is as you knew at age nine, camouflage. Life is not as it appears. Life is not as it seems.

The presuming people do here, eyes telling them what they see is real. Ears telling them what they hear is real. All assume this is real. They pretend, they juggle and they find ways to justify. It is not so! All are in the school of the little self, the school of the ego. This ego-school to graduate from is to embrace and acknowledge the real self and the reality is the cornflower's lesson of real, a point of light everlasting.

The Holy, loving and created self-loved, unchanged, unchanging, eternally keeps by him who is real in a heaven that's for all as one.

One thing that will strike you is that it said Jesus is an ordinary guy like every kind of person you know.

A kind and caring soul who incarnated into human pajamas and was able to bi-locate all over the world becoming Caucasian, Hebrew, Chinese, black, blue, green, and yellow depending on the time and need for his teaching, a dedicated spirit who came here to show us how to think on things that are important.

Yes. Oh yes. Not God in disguise for sure!

Yes, you understood that early on too but your problem was much deeper in a way. You had, after much consideration starting at age thirteen, no belief in anything or anyone, an absolute atheist, you will for the next twenty-seven years be a truly lost soul. Nothing you study will help at all and you will read and study all major religions, great thinkers and Bible philosophers. You name it, you studied it, and were baptized in the Catholic Church admitting it was conditional because you only wanted to believe but most assuredly did not! In many ways that is always a living hell.

You would like to be able to embrace that.

Yes, I am reminded of the Tibetan Master Longchempa's statement made in the fourteenth century: "Since things neither exist nor don't exist, are neither real nor unreal, are utterly beyond adopting and rejecting. We might as well burst out laughing!"

⊶ ≖◆≖ ⊷

Once upon a time in a small dusty town, there lived a little family; Father Joseph, a village carpenter, Mary the mother and some children. One of the children was called Jeshua, later referred to as "Jeshua of Nazareth." He too was a carpenter like his father. He was also a stonemason. Indeed, he was a fine craftsman in his village that like many others sold their wares to merchants on the trade routes near their town. Jeshua was also a teacher. He taught in quiet words to whoever would listen that caring, love and loyalty, goodness and integrity are the ways to greet life each morning.

Jeshua of Nazareth was a Jew. His dark, slightly curly hair hung to his shoulders. He had dark eyes and darkish skin. He was not tall, perhaps five-nine or less, and of slight build. He was strong though and his hands showed that he was a workman, firm and nimble. He smiled a lot and his eyes were kind. If you had a big brother, you would want your big brother to be like Jeshua.

On a pleasant day in June, a very, very long time ago, a group of townspeople were chatting near a well on the edge of their town. The well was a common meeting place for exchanging news and collecting jugs of water for the day.

Jeshua was there and several of the children tugged on his brown tunic and pleaded with him to tell them a story. So, he did.

"Let's sit here and say the Lord's Prayer together first, shall we? And, then I will tell you a story."

The people gathered around him, the children in front, and one little dark-eyed girl about age five sat on his lap. We will call her Eva. She held a small red apple in her hand.

Our Father: "Yes," he said. "Our Father is who God is and God loves us."

Who art in heaven: "Yes," Jeshua said again. "And we are with our Father God in a home created for us called Heaven. Only for a little bit we have forgotten that we are there with our Father God."

Hallowed be thy name and again Jeshua said, "Yes, God's name is indeed holy and sacred, hallowed and in truth we do not say God's holy name, we just know God is God."

Thy Kingdom come once more Jeshua paused and said, "God's Kingdom is always God's Kingdom and we share that Kingdom with God forever and ever."

Thy will be done "God's will is God's intent to love us for all eternity," Jeshua said to the gathering crowd by the well.

On earth and for the tiniest little second, the small girl on Jeshua's lap tried to bite a piece of her red apple. Alas, as is true of most five year old, she had no teeth and a bite of apple was simply impossible. Jeshua looked down at her smiling and said: "Eva, not to worry. In the Heaven God creates for us there are lovely apples and your front teeth are all grown in with no gaps at all! Does that please you?"

Eva smiled back at Jeshua as though he were her big strong brother who knew all things. And, the Lord's Prayer continued to be said at the well in the dusty town of Nazareth in a country far, far away in a time so long ago we almost remember not.

And we are all in that kindergarten class by the well.

In less time than it takes Eva to think to try a tiny bite of her apple was the thought of separateness and individuality, of egos and worlds and universes, of trains and puppies and toucans and doctors! That came into being; gone, never happened.

It took far less "time" than Eva's little intent of a bite and all that was seemingly made in billions and billions of earth years and a big bang. Artifacts and old bones, the horns in heaven never missed a single grace note. That which we call earth, life, our unreal imaginary "magic" illusion of what we call our lives never happened in that single less than fragment of Eva's intent. Nothing happened!

And, the Lord's Prayer continues **as it is in Heaven**.

And this is what prepared Dolly for her adult life.

At age thirty-seven, Dolly was shown a door leading to what seemed a cellar, or crypt actually, and asked to go through the door and spend an entire night in the most pitch black, agonizing, horrifically depressing place any imagination could conjure up. It started about one-thirty in the morning and the depth and weight of it released her as dawn crept over the east woods.

It was a dawning burned into her very soul. The agony faded and she was once again seeing a new day.

Oh, the realization of nothingness and no way out, the sorrow and lack of hope of ever being free, the stark terror and lack of joy she can recall even now though it feels far removed. She never again suffered such since that fateful night in this life, no matter the turns and twists of the dream and tears and grief. Yes, sensitive and aware to a marked degree, but none to compare to that hopelessness and black despair.

Jeshua said he taught what he felt might be accepted. He spent most of his time, however, being one of the common traders and merchants of his time and listening and learning of them. He truly was one of them. His offerings were suited to the time and the ability of the people he met. To listen to him, and he was chary of what he taught, careful and simple, he talked to common people after an evening meal or during a time of illness or walking to the well, ordinary, commonplace, not noticeable. That is the only way to teach; one offers and then slips away. But that was too simple for those who created the Jesus story.

These are the lessons Jeshua taught Dolly, just as predicted by Muffy:

Lesson One:

There are no divisions. In reality no division in Heaven, all is one. God is God. We are created in God's image and there is no place where God stops and we begin. We are created like unto God. There is no Jeshua, who is the second person of the Holy Trinity. There is no Holy Trinity. There is no Holy Spirit, the third person of the Holy Trinity. Those words are used to convey to us a way that we might understand at least a little.

Jesus was in history; a man not a God. He is as much but no more than we are: God's created one.

The Jesus personality was just that, a human personality dressed in human pajamas and he left this dream world on a cross. He did not suffer. He knew beyond all of us that it was an illusion he was involved in. He was so very wise and he knew about our dreaming days (and nights) long before he chose a body to chat with his fellow Jews on the trade routes. He did not get sucked into the silly dream stuff we are in as we hop about on our stage.

Jesus is a symbol for wanting only good for others. He did not value his body any more than we need to value ours. He knew who he is and he knew who we are: spirit choosing a body for a time of years, dream time that spans lifetimes in time terms but are all one at the same time. And, all are dream and never happened! We must forgive our foolish thinking that it did happen and, thus, forgive ourselves and everyone else for such erroneous thinking.

All that was important to him was to love one another. And, yes there was more but he chose his audience carefully and he never gave or offered more than his friends could handle. Much of what is attributed to him never happened.

Jeshua, from our point of view, comes from a far place, a different realm than three dimensions. He chose to come and partake of human life on planet earth, just as Dolly chose to leave Erra.

God is mind. We are mind. Holy Spirit is a symbol of the memory of God within each one of us. A way for us to re-remember that we are God's created one when we are able at some point to grasp the concept.

The "Christian" world uses Jeshua as a symbol of God's love and then proceeds to elevate his body to a status that he intended not at all. "Christians" have done some pretty amazing things and embraced some pretty far-out beliefs about Jeshua! He is a symbol for goodness, period.

Now Heaven is our home where we never left, unchanging, unchanged, and eternal. We are dreaming. All eventually in time terms awaken to the truth that we dream. When we awaken we can pretend, we can go back to sleep, we can embrace all manner of ego-oriented stances but the fact is that once we realize, truly realize that we are dreaming, we know. From that moment on, although we may slip backward every other moment, we do know! And then we must, simply must, live with the intent to be compassionate and live with the realization that we do adopt a life-pattern that reflects our best. And, that other self is "not too shabby" a way to conduct our life.

—— ◅◆▻ ——

Now in order to live the life of awake, it is necessary to understand how mind, which is God and which we are, can be so foolish as to think it could separate itself from a perfect home in a perfect heaven. That is the most foolish notion ever conceived to be sure. Well, the answer is it could not happen. It is impossible, yet here we believe we are and this most assuredly is not heaven.

It is small comfort to accept that nothing ever happened to those of us within the dream, awake or not, who believe we are pretty solid blood, sweat, and tears. So to try, and this is trying only to give a reasonable answer, it is needful to say that, although it did not and could not happen, here we are, or seem to believe we are, in this "too, too solid flesh." Though John Ruskin said, "When love and skill work together expect a masterpiece."

There is mind and mind determines what bodies do, not the other way around. For simplicity's sake, and no other, the mind is dumbed down by agreement in physical reality so we will explore and search and solve the mysteries we agree to meet when we incarnate. We do not bring all our true wisdom with us when we take on blue eyes and brown hair, black skin, gender, illness, etc.; our agreement in incarnations is to look for answers. Some incarnate with more of themselves than others but basically we come in fairly unknowing. For the sake of understanding, divide as you think about this, mind into something like parcels. The dreamer chooses a part (and there are no parts!) of mind to make decisions in this duality level in which we find ourselves, believing we are here. This parceling of the mind has been referred to by Kenneth Wapnick, who writes about *A Course in Miracles* as the decision maker. It's a useful way to describe what we as dreamers do. We appropriate a portion of the mind for our dream purposes. We ignore the rest in our dreams. We use a portion to conduct our lives in our dreams and we choose the decisions we make in our moments. Remember, the real mind is God and ours by right as he created.

However, we choose to "forget" all or most of that and we make up a way to keep our dreams going by having a made-up part of us, an ego. The ego makes choices and some of our choices leave much to be desired, as we all well know. Those choices are made in what we call the arena of free will and it does seem as though we have free will. However, keep in mind this very important statement. All never happened. All is completed and never was so within that tiny nothing. What I call nothing is no more than a "gray dandelion parachute blown by the sly north wind." Not even that much happened. In fact, nothing ever happened at all. All decisions, all galaxies, all time and space, worlds and universes and all images and forms and whatever nothings happened in that brief, less than an instant blowing in the wind, actually never happened. We just think that all this happened or is happening. Only we think in error. We believe in error. We insist on our error because that keeps good old ego center stage and ongoing.

All that is, God, Heaven, us, is as it has ever been and will ever be, and untouched by time and space and bodies and whatever. God is in Heaven. So we are eternally, full stop. There is no anything else. Reality is Heaven. All else is illusion, made up, a stage we make called our life and we all act out our parts from a script we ourselves write each seeming moment.

We gain in understanding in our dream focus, we allow more of mind to show forth to our dream-self. Instead of stamping our sneakered foot in indignation about wanting to be me, me, me, we push our intense ego-self off the stage, usually bit by bit into obscurity behind the stage props, out behind the potted plants and we allow the mind which is ever ours to shine forth as self, and self is other. We are all one. This usually takes time and often many lifetimes in dream terms to realize. When we awaken, the mind is ours to use in a manner that can be called our real mind, God's intent for us as his creation in heaven. God, our creator, knows nothing of worlds and bodies and rape and pillage and sunsets and baby ducks. God is God, Heaven is Heaven and we are in Heaven with God. That is reality. There is nothing other than reality.

Do we get the whole enchilada? The whole mind here in dream? No, we do not. If we did, most of us would disintegrate in an instant. We could not bear the eternal joy and could not endure the perfectness. So we get glimpses, we get messages, we get inklings, we get assistance to see, and we get moments of joy beyond joy. But, there are few who could bear up and remain in this dimension; there are no dimensions! Those are words if all of mind were at our disposal in the bodies we trot about in.

So, ours is in a sense metered mind and the "cloud of unknowing" is to bring us on to maturity but not overwhelm us. And when all is understood and we have gained insight, we laugh and laugh and laugh and laugh at our foolishness that anything could be other than our perfect home with God in Heaven.

On Healing: You do not heal others. It is not possible. You offer thoughts, ideas, energy, and prayer if you like that work as a gift for another to accept or not as the other chooses. We do not heal one another. We offer a path to use our love if an other accepts. That is healing.

Yes, we are mind and mind is free to make choices to indicate what and who we are at the ego-dream level. We have the ability to discern between ego and non-ego. The dream level is duality, the moment-to-moment obligation to choose, give or take, offer or keep, run or walk, love or hate. Those choices indicate whether we are living, awake, and choosing love and forgiveness for the silly thought that we could be other than love or we choose the ego's path of: I want what I want when I want it and you better move over if you are in my way. Then, of course, there are all the moment to moment "almost love or almost ego" decisions. Even so here we are with that age-old "decisions-decisions" impetus built into the dream-level. So we choose, like it or not, we choose. Even fence sitting is a choice and each personality who is the dreamer makes choices, which show clearly what we are learning in the now.

◆━ ≍✦≍ ━◆

Lesson Two:

Yes, we "lucid dream and affect as best we can" but to those who love, love, love their individuality and their separateness, to say that, not only is all dream but personalities and uniqueness and indeed the very self we identify as Moi is a dreamer dreaming and not real scares the life out of most everyone. They howl and run or defend like mad or pronounce such thoughts to be lunatic.

To be one, the idea is nearly unfathomable as we are focused now. One? All as One? That is reality, but it is so hard to understand and then bring back and find words and to hear verbally that form and matter. And stuff is all made up and not real. It is a hellish nightmare to anyone who dares to peek over the edge of the seeming abyss of: "What in the hell will happen to me? Will I be gone, evaporated, dismissed, unattended, ignored bypassed, or not there?" Yep all of that and more. "You jest ain't what you think you is."

⊷ ▰✦▱ ⊶

You, dear one, may think it's easy to see how the above can be. Well, it is not easy for most. They want their candy store intact, putting out nice pieces of fudge and fruities on the counter for all to see and admire. The understanding that things are not as they appear is so scary that running in the opposite direction and holding one's ears is the only way to escape such horror. That's the strength of the ego and intense is a puny word for the dogged determination and even viciousness to which the ego will turn in order to have its priceless self center stage and reciting its lines with every spotlight on. It is deadly horrific for any ego to consider such and to muster the strength to hear; it is a huge requirement of willingness and patience. But it simply means we have to do lucid dreaming and affect the dream as best we can. Yes, all lives are dreams and all are being dreamed. Now what seems to us like eons of what we measure as time is but the tiniest flick of an ash, a mere moment that has no duration at all.

———— ⊱✦⊰ ————

The word "karma" has connotations of a series of lives that could be visualized as beads on a rosary, a trail in a seemingly endless path. Not so. All lives are now like stacked games of chess, like pancakes one atop the other and like Oreo® cookie sandwiches. All lives are in this nano-second of what we could call the "Tool of Time" (Julian Barbour).

That being said, karma is how we resolve various lessons we give to ourselves in our dream lives. Messing about in Peter's life means Paul will have some explaining to do with and for Peter in other dream circumstances all being worked out and resolved now. Our brains, as we have them more or less securely in our heads, are receptive to what our minds determine for us and can more or less deal with this seeming now, i.e. get out of bed, dream our day. The mind sees all our lives as one. This brain has all it can do to deal with what we perceive in this body's

brain as "a day in the life of…" We just cannot manage that kind
of computer stacking.

If there is no time, there is no time. We make it as a capable
tool so we can manage our dream-life in physical three-dimensional non-reality. We would use a screwdriver to fix the screen
door or an automobile to take us to Grandma's house at Thanks-
giving and all happened already. Yes, all of time is already over
and never began as it is all dreams. Ideas remain with the author
of the idea. We perceive a world out there but that is a projection
of our thoughts and not real. We are God's creation as one and as
such we are unchanged, unchanging, and eternal. All else is dream
and does not exist. There can be nothing, literally nothing, outside perfection. We can think and believe and act as if. Our dreams
are real and it's likely best we do just that. We just cannot sit on a
curb in Kansas and declare, "I am done with this dream. It's all
not real and I will sit here until I quit dreaming." Denial does not
work. We are choosing dreaming so let's dream with some measure of panache and dignity and a standard of behavior befitting
a human who takes responsibility for one's own dream.

All is now. All is long over and never began. All is make-
believe and made up. All lives are now and the you in each of

the dreams you now dream. The now knows the dream you seem to be living is a focus. You are choosing this life dream to relive. How can that be? The analogy of an orange covered with different colored map pins with each pin representing a life dream change of Dolly. The you called Norm this time or Peter, Paul, or Perry. The names change. You do not. You are in each map pin now on the orange that is the you composite.

You, Dolly, choose the "red Dolly map-pin" in the twentieth/twenty-first century. That map pin, Dolly, in the now is very much as though when you choosing that map pin and unraveling this seeming life as Dolly becomes a video of this now focused Dolly as a lifetime. You choose the map-pin. When examining it closely it becomes a video from a shelf of "map-pin Dollies" which you are choosing to replay. It has all been lived and all played all over and never begun. All is a dream. Thus the fretting about karma has been resolved in all your now lives, in the pancake and chess games you have as your basket of Norm and Peter and Paul and Perry and...

We select a video-life to replay and when we drop our drawers in 3D, we go to Summerland and choose another map-pin video to replay or if I, Dolly, decide to no longer be the "map-pin video-playing Dolly," I then realize I am in Heaven where I never left. Or maybe others choose other dream realities to replay, refocus on, relive. All are free to choose to dream endlessly or to choose the life of perfection in Heaven where we all are as one and where dreams never happened and could never happen because there is nothing, as in "nothing outside" of perfection.

All is resolved in one or many of your map-pin lives on the orange of you. Sit for a moment on Venus in loving attention and view your orange covered with map-pins who are your seemingly endless you. Zoom in on that particular red map pin you as Dolly in this minute, see how it plays very like a video before your very eyes, observer and observed and player. Absorbed I am in being Dolly immersed in the focused Dolly who is reading this exchange. Finish reading and turn to lunch. Finish lunch and note your day/night/days/years/work/pleasure/etc. That is map-pin red Dolly involved with her dream video in this now.

←•→ ⊠⊹⊠ ←•→

Sit for a moment on Mars in rapt attention as you do the above in a life of Peter. I shall not detail. You know it well that life too is playing out the video life of dream. Only your attention is not focused there in this now. You are focused here with me as we exchange thoughts but that blue map-pin Dolly or that one named Peter are just as much a dream. You in any life are working out that life just as you are in this focus bits and bobs at a "time." We are slow, in earth "time." (Hence David Hawkins' insistence that most of humanity is at 190 on a scale of one to a thousand.) Even so, in the large picture as you sit on Mars looking over the broad view, all is now.

All is from our human brain outlook barely able to cope with this seeming dream moment, let alone an orange covered with dream map-pins. We just cannot so we pick and choose and replay and maintain our beloved individuality and uniqueness by choosing dreaming so we can freely be you and me. Yes, we do love our individual dreams. We seem to love them, do we not? Here we are focused on our stage and with our actors and the script at the ready. Yet all is resolved. All is completed. All is played. All is not and never was.

＋—＝＋＝—＋

You are indeed free to choose how to dream the remainder of this seeming life (and all other lives of yours that are all now). God did not make this world, worlds, and universes. God did not make us. God has no caring about dreams that never happened! God knows we are in eternity, in bliss as one. The Heaven where God dwells is our home.

＋—＝＋＝—＋

We make our dream world. We project from our mind a world and its contents. Then we proceed to react to the world we make.

It's all made up. It's a magic show. It's make-believe. It is a matter of individual choosing. Each is free to live, choose, find whatever is wise and right and best in the moment for them. By choosing, over many lifetimes, we gain understanding and we gain wisdom and we gain awareness, hopefully, even though Hawkins on his scale of one to ten says we are mighty slow learners.

* * *

Teachers offer ideas: It's a bit like passing a tray of chocolate cookies at a party. Some there exclaim, "Oh yes please! My favorite kind of cookie! I will enjoy it immensely." Others never look up to see what you are offering. They are too busy talking or whatever. Others say, "No thank you. I prefer lemon drops." Others take a bite and put the cookie on the table. Others put two in their pocket or purse for later. And, some grab the entire tray and say, "Here, let me help you pass these about. I know there are many here who will find this very much to their liking. Some will surely want your recipe."

We each make every tiny nano-second of the dream we are focused on. So the "how long and how much" depends on the individual; some for seemingly endless lifetimes and some perhaps a few laughs and but a tiny tick of a clock. There is no answer. Humanity itself and all of us together pull ourselves out of the mire of ego-centered existence in dreams that appear to wind on to infinity. It need not be so.

What has to happen is frank and personal. You choose to see. You choose to hear. You choose to act from this day forward. This is not will power and not pig-headed determination. Rather it is a "Here I stand and refuse to go on as I have been." You seize this moment and will henceforth pay attention. You are no longer blind and deaf. You are no longer accepting such a poor stage performance. You shall learn your lines and deliver them with elegance and awareness. You shall learn your craft. You shall be and reflect to any who pass your door that your actions and thoughts and words reflect the real you, the you that you choose to be.

⊷ ⊰⊹⊱ ⊶

This is a grave and serious place to stand to be sure because if carried through moment to moment, it is a lifelong dedication at one and the same time. No over-seriousness, laughing and being silly over a weak moment. No being astonished at great lapses. No being downcast when the life we make seems so unlike what we are determined to have in our viewfinder. No sullen, cranky disgust when nothing but nothing seems to indicate we are getting more like the true loving self. Usually after such a determined line is drawn in the sand, we grow worse instead of better.

Life seems to take such a downturn we can despair easily. Weeping and gnashing of teeth are common. What is happening is not at all that. What is really happening is that we have dared to open our eyes wider. The curtains are drawn back a wee bit and there escapes from our inner self the scream, "Am I truly that far from what I choose to be?"

In truth, of course, we are and that is but the beginning. Even so, it is a beginning. After a lifelong choice, no matter what, until that is the path we trot and it seems as though we are wallowing in muck to our waist. Yet when we finally really see, in whatever lifetime, it was a mere puddle to step over and not the Grand Canyon at all. It is a very difficult choice to be awake and aware and to be that person we choose to be.

Pond skimming is an external way to make amends and there is no doubt whatever that is helpful to many, certainly to those who can be somewhat mollified by that kind of amend-making. Deny nothing regarding the advantage of doing something toward erasing and cleaning up one's acts. If Hail Marys can do that, then by all means more Hail Marys.

⇥✦⇤

Fear not. You are loved eternally and you are worthy. Be then who you are each moment of your life. Each and every moment be that person. It will take a lifetime to practice the qualities of who you are each moment. It requires never not knowing you can be that. It requires never not knowing you are awake and aware; it requires not less than all of you and done in a way that is amusing, witty and joyously knowing that person will not emerge overnight. It takes time for a caterpillar to become the butterfly and there is nothing wrong with caterpillars as long as the butterfly is the goal.

→→ ☰✦☰ ←←

We can have as many "Shards of the Mirror" as we choose. It is our dream. All is now. There are no dimensions. That is a group of words, which we use to help our brains sort things out. It's dreamtime. All dreams seem to us, the dreamers, to be real. They are not. All ideas and concepts we dream up are usually a numbers game to keep the mystery of the dream and egos alive and well and trotting on stage to give their lines. All dreams are the dreamer's way of not admitting that the only reality is heaven. All aspects of dreams are projections from the dreamer's mind and projections are not real. They are projections. Dreamers dream whatever they choose to dream. Male and female have meaning only in our dreams. In reality it is Heaven. There are no divisions of any kind.

All is one, and quite at peace!

Fear and Disquiet

The dream world can be and often is a loud and greedy place, filled with "the wants of ego." Others' egos as well as your own.

Peace and inner quiet must be your center. Then no matter what crashes about your ears in the din of three dimensions, all remains without. Then and only then is it possible to maintain that dear quiet place within, which is your true self.

To help you find your center choose for a time your dog, your barn, your woods; the grassy places and a brook rippling over stones, those are helpful but not of course essential.

Fear is a sadness of ages, admittedly all now, however, convictions steeped like tea in time, allow not other than sadness and fear to be den brothers. In sorrow. Allow them to deliver their lines and give them their walking papers and see them stumble back among the potted palms.

Empty the stage. The audience goes home. Strike the set and that play is done, once for all.

Freedom from fear means freedom from the tiniest vestiges of any threads that linger to bring you away from your true living place in this dream-world.

Your send fear packing. You send disquiet packing. You quietly remain you amidst whatever. It is an act of courage and bravery to insist they return not into your dream.

Run, walk, trot, jog. Stand or crawl. Do whatever it takes to avail yourself of the freedom to choose not fear. Then you are available to inner silence and peace. Then the avenue of freedom from the tyranny of three dimension is your own. You alone can make it so.

In Stillness

Remember how the sun swept west in summer at the farm?
Remember the star in the west sky burnt blue after dinner?
You came singing the song of you.
We were warm, you remember?
Our lives touched as one, asking nothing.
Asking everything.
I have sat her long and longer still—
Remembering our answers.
And they were sweet, kind and yes, star swept
Have you forgotten the brown-eyed susans?
In your field of going away
Have you then taken your summer self to a place beyond?
A place where I grow tired as trespasser
And still know not where you dwell.
You have then a guarded cover
Holding hard-won lines of you that are become
—dream-dust?
The lesson is: ***This is a dream. There is no time.***
Forgive all. Love.* Awaken *to the reality of Heaven.

Personal Ponies, Ltd., Inc.

Mission Statement: "What is real magic?"

Personal Ponies, Ltd., is a not-for profit organization founded in 1986 to promote the idea that children with disabilities will be immeasurably enriched by having a small pony to care for and enjoy. Personal Ponies Ltd. will place ponies free in the homes of children with disabilities. Personal Ponies Ltd. will also place free ponies in Therapeutic Riding Schools and Child Day Care Centers. Personal Ponies Ltd. intends continuing interest in both pony and child for the duration of their relationship in the form of personal visits from volunteer members of Personal Ponies Ltd. in addition to other forms of communication.

Vision Statement

The vision of Personal Ponies, Ltd., is:

• To achieve national acceptance and respect for the idea that a small pony and a child with disabilities can have a relationship of lasting value.

• To expect involvement by Foundations, business people and private citizens on the National, State and local levels

• To encourage integrity and continuous improvement in the development of a nationwide network for the placement of Personal Ponies for children with disabilities.

• To unite the efforts of agencies previously organized for the disabled and to utilize their expertise for reaching, evaluating and endorsing the placement of ponies offered by Personal Ponies Ltd..

—➤ ▰✦▰ ◆—

Fundamantal Objectives

• To maintain the integrity of Personal Ponies Ltd. by the establishment and enforcement of procedures for validation of all monetary donations, pony donations and product donations using computer-based records for all transactions.

• To develop a program to improve the concept of the value of small ponies for children with disabilities through education, funded advertising and the personal participation of interested persons.

• To establish careful rules for maintaining ponies in a proper manner and to educate persons involved with the ponies about careful and correct management practices.

• To promote the idea that nondisabled youth can and should be involved with the Personal Ponies Ltd. program.

• To create a greater public awareness of the concept of Personal Ponies Ltd. and the importance of children with disabilities enjoying a small pony as a form of life enrichment.

• The use of an aggressive advertising program and effective education programs such as videos and films, T-shirts and other pertinent products.

• To develop long-range planning using experts in many fields with careful consideration given to the idea of funding research for the greater understanding of the kinship of human and equine.

⇥⬧⇤

"Think on These Things"

Guidelines for Administrators

1. Personal Ponies Ltd., Inc., retains life ownership of all ponies.

2. Health review and updates of each pony, using official form, including name, address and phone number of attending qualified veterinarian, to be presented to State Directors by Community Directors in December of each year.

3. State Directors are responsible for appointing Community Directors in their states, State Directors to instruct candidates regarding job description and program expectations prior to all Community Director appointments.

4. State and Community Directors together appoint pony sponsors and determine pony placement with families having differently able children. The Central Office to be informed by Regional and State Directors concerning program activities.

5. State Directors together with Community Directors and the National Director of Breeding and Placement (and Assistant) determine the choice of volunteer breeding farms.

6. Ponies in the program are to be humanely euthanized

and a death certificate issued by the attending veterinarian. The death certificate to be sent to the Central Office. A Community Director together with the attending veterinarian determines this action when there is no longer "Quality of Life."

7. After one warning a Community Director has the authority to remove any pony whose caretaker does not adhere to program expectations or whose daily care does not PPL standards.

8. Personal Ponies is organized as a team approach program. Regional and State Directors are expected to communicate regularly with the National Director. Community Directors are to communicate regularly with State Directors who are to be readily available. Community Directors are to meet with and communicate regularly with the volunteer members in their communities.

9. The Personal Ponies breeding program is primarily aimed toward the breeding of quality United Kingdom Shetlands of small and midi sizes using carefully selected foundation stock. This is a process, and a primary goal.

10. All members are urged to contact the Central Office for additional information and/or clarification of written guidelines.

The United Kingdom Shetland Pony

The Shetland Islands are situated about a hundred miles off the north coast of Scotland. Only a few of the large group of islands are inhabited as the land is poor and unproductive. How much environment has had to do with the size and character of the ponies there and whether they are from original Shetland stock remains a question with no possibility of a definite conclusion to be offered. It is my belief that prior to the division of the great northern land mass into islands and island groups the wild Celtic ponies roamed freely and it is only in comparatively recent historic times that unique and distinct breeds have developed such as the Norwegian Dun, Icelandic, Highland, Welsh, Shetland and other Mountain Moorland pony breeds unique to the United Kingdom.

Shetland ponies have long existed under most adverse conditions. They have been close companions of the natives of the islands sharing their huts and food. The ponies I saw in the U.K. are all characterized by diminutive size, hardiness, and good dispositions, without exception. They are accustomed to scarce grazing and without a doubt over countless generations this lack of food accounts for their small size.

The Shetland is of a small draft-horse in type and gives the maximum of horsepower in the smallest package. They are not used for farm work as such, though they have long been used for draft purposes in the coal and tin mines of Scotland, Wales and in the mines of Kentucky, Tennessee and West Virginia until such time as the mines became mechanized. An old miner told me that his grandfather was employed by the colliers to strike the mine ponies' eyes with a hammer. The eyes were then sewn shut to eliminate the concern for coal dust infections…after all, who needs eyes during a thirty-year stay in the black depths of the coal mines! A sad commentary on our often inhumane treatment of animals.

In spite of their diminutive size, they are able to draw half a ton of coal and cover twenty to thirty miles a day. Shetlands are wonderful weight-carriers too. A Shetland three feet in height is able to carry a full-grown man on his back for long distances. (Not exactly my idea of how a small pony deserves to be treated; however, I was assured this was common practice and still is so on the islands.) The crofters use the Shetlands for packing peat and their customary load is 120 to 140 pounds. This is remarkable when it is considered that the average height of these ponies is thirty-six to forty inches. (No Shetland may be included in the Shetland Pony Stud Book, which exceeds forty-two inches in height at age four.)

Considering his weight and height, the Shetland is the winner in the draft horse world. In addition, the Shetland's ability to work under the stress of weather conditions and insufficient food, it is obvious that the Shetland pony has no peer in the equine working world.

It is now the custom to give the ponies rations of hay in severe weather, and that allays the losses due to starvation. I was told in Scotland when surrounded by nineteen black stallions on a mountainside that "they are hard as ten-penny nails come February and that keeps the breed hardy. The less capable just don't make it."

Conditions on the islands are little different from that of their Shetland forebears, a bleak and nearly shelter-less life in work; or when not working they spend their time foraging here and there for wisps of dried grasses and weeds. They are known to eat dead fish and certainly kelp. I was told they pile their dung, and early on the foals are taught to do the same. In lean years, they use their heaped dung-piles as a means to survive. It has been my observation that Shetlands eat more salt than other breeds. Perhaps due to centuries of eating salty kelp? My own preference for feeding Celtic breeds is a gray salt, which can be purchased or ordered in a natural foods store.

Shetlands on the mainland often receive better rations and better forage than Island Shetlands. Educated breeding practices on the mainland (and to a limited extent on the islands) have created a consistent standard size Shetland of outstanding quality in the forty to forty-two inch size, retaining all the admirable qualities of the ancient Shetland as to bone and sturdiness and, of course, that impeccable temperament. Small Shetlands are often of lesser quality though some breeders of the

smaller ponies have carefully bred small and midi sizes. Those
are the sizes in which the Personal Ponies organization is most
interested. I do see a future time, perhaps in the next century,
when the Standard Shetland size pony would be most useful
for differently able children who are older and/or capable physically of handling a larger pony. This is not of current interest
to the PPL program.

In Scotland, herds of Shetlands (I saw mostly black ponies)
were grazing the mountainsides with black-face sheep. I was
told that the ponies keep the mountain paths open for the sheep
during severe snows. The ponies push the stones and rocks to
find tender roots and grasses and in a primitive way, this must
to some extent till the mountain soil.

Black is the accepted color for Shetlands. There are bays
and browns and now and again chestnuts; few grays and rarely
a colored Shetland of outstanding quality to match the blacks.
I saw in my travels in the U.K. only two colored individuals it
would have been my joy to bring home. Piebalds and Skewbalds
are seen commonly on the islands and it seems they are much
sought after by children. (It is my experience that most any kind
of pony looks good to a child wanting a "pony of my very own."

Judgment is required to a great degree in the quest for Shetlands suited for importing and to be used in our PPL breeding
program. Temperament must be our first consideration. I am

happy to say that, without exception, my contacts with Shetlands in the U.K. afforded me the conviction that every Shetland pony I met is of a kindly and affable disposition. I cannot tell you the pleasure it gives to me to report this is so! Their docile natures enable them to put up with the whims of children without resentment or rebellion. In fact, they seemed to genuinely enjoy children in every way regardless of a loud child voice or a headstall that fell over a pony eye! I can truly say that I was entranced by their intelligence, their patience and their singular attitude of enjoyment in the hands of their little people...and yes it was a love affair. The realization that I had indeed found the pony I was seeking for the children in the Personal Ponies program was a great joy to me.

Few Shetlands have what is called saddle-horse conformation. There is some discussion about an Oriental Type Shetland, possibly the influence of a small Arabian stallion used on the Island of Fetlar to improve the quality of the native ponies. I found nothing substantial to believe that, as in any breed, there are what for want of a better term individuals called and preferred what is termed: "Londonderry." A blocky, short legged, wide-bodied pony. He is short-backed and heavy boned, has heavy thighs, gaskins, arms all of which indicated to me a pony of great strength for comparative size. A pony suited by temperament and type to be the companion and friend of a differently able child, indeed any child! A child's pony suitable for a pony ride. A pony never to be outgrown because he has the stout and hefty body capable of pulling a carriage with an adult and a child aboard. A pony for all ages in fact. A pony to fill what I like to think is the equine version of the story of "The Velveteen Rabbit," the United Kingdom Shetland pony.

———•———

The United Kingdom Shetland Pony

Prancing feet and curtain mane,
Jaunty style—he's never plain.
Bone and substance ample there
Style and action sweet and fair.
Noble eye and handsome head
Sturdy, bold and yes, well bred.
Solid neck and shoulder laid
See then how handsome this pony's made.
Short-legged and strong with frame well knit,
See the Shetland, watch him go
To child, the stud or to a show.
Short of back and ribs well sprung,
Sound of limb and sound of lung.
Strength of loin and quarters wide,
With grace and majesty he's allied.
Pony power living pleasure
The Shetland
Child's friend forever (7-200)

(written in honor of "Highlands Cupid," stallion donated
to PPL by Melissa Warren, Kimross, Scotland, and in memory
of Cupid's brother "Highfields Dylan")

PPL Commandments of Leadership

(Recommended Management Philosophy)

1. People are often illogical, often unreasonable and often self-centered. We are required to love them anyway. And serve them.

2. Doing good means we will often be accused of selfish and ulterior motives. We are required to do good anyway.

3. It is quite possible that the good done today will be forgotten by tomorrow. We will do good anyway.

4. Success often brings with it false friends and true enemies. No matter, we will succeed anyway.

5. Being candid and honest make us vulnerable. We will be both candid and honest.

6. The biggest of us with the biggest of ideas can be shot down by the smallest of us with the smallest minds. We will think big anyway.

7. Most people favor underdogs but follow top dogs. We will not forget to champion the underdogs.

8. What we spend years building can be destroyed overnight. Build anyway.

9. People often need help and may well attack if helped. Help anyway.

10. We will give people in this world the best that we have to give. Once in awhile we will get kicked in the teeth. We will give the people in this world the best we have anyway.

Personal Ponies, Ltd.

Personal Ponies began with the dream of our founder, Marianne Alexander (and just two ponies) to do something special for special kids. As a breeder of Connemara Ponies and Irish Sport Horses for more than thirty years, she wanted to give something back, and when she discovered the incredible sensitivity of the UK Shetland Pony to children with disabilities, and saw firsthand how they changed children's lives, she knew what she had to do.

Our mission is to make *magic* in children's lives, to bring smiles and joy in a most unusual way. We believe (and we've seen it happen over and over again) that the lives of children with special needs are immeasurably enriched by having a small equine companion to love and care for, so this is what we do! Our ponies are uniquely suited in temperament and size to small children, and we provide them to families completely without charge, our version of the Velveteen Rabbit.

Thanks to the tireless energy of Marianne, PPL has grown into a national organization involving hundreds of volunteers throughout the country. We now have programs in almost every state, and have placed ponies with many hundreds of children, and hundreds more are on our waiting list. We depend on both the hearts and hands of hundreds of volunteer breeders, promoters, and sponsors, as well as those who support us financially, so that we can continue to grow and serve children who need something special in their lives.

Would you like to know how you can help?

Please spend some time with us. Find out why we breed UK Shetlands and read stories about our kids and their ponies. Join our e-mail chat list and get to know the people who are active in our community. Subscribe to our free, online newsletter to find out more about our activities. Read about our volunteer program and our unique breeding program. Check out our list of State Directors and contact us to see what you can do to help in your community.

If you are able, please make a financial contribution. You can be assured that one hundred percent of your funds will go directly to supporting our program. The demand for ponies far exceeds our ability to provide them. Our list of children with special needs waiting for their very own "Personal Pony" is long. We need you!

All royalties from *Pony Wisdom for the Soul* go to Personal Ponies.

www.personalponies.org

personalponies@earthlink.net

About Dr. C. Norman Shealy

C. Norman Shealy, M.D., Ph.D., is a neurosurgeon, trained at Massachusetts General Hospital, after medical school at Duke University. He has taught at Harvard, Western Reserve, the University of Wisconsin, the University of Minnesota, and Forest Institute of Professional Psychology. Currently he is President of Holos University Graduate Seminary (www.holosuniversity. org).

In 1978, Dr. Shealy was instrumental in creating the American Holistic Medical Association, which continues to emphasize the spiritual component of healing. He was the founding president of AHMA for its first two years.

In 1973, recognizing the need to incorporate spirituality into medical practice, he founded, with Reverend Henry Rucker, the Science of Mind Church of Chicago, which became the International Science of Mind Church for Spiritual Healing, and which created Holos University Graduate Seminary, offering masters and doctoral programs in Spiritual Healing and Energy Medicine.

Dr. Shealy introduced the concepts of Dorsal Column Stimulation and Transcutaneous Electrical Nerve Stimulation (TENS), both now used worldwide. This innovation has led to the establishment of international societies dedicated to furthering the field

*of neuromodulation. In 1971 he founded the first comprehensive,
holistic clinic for management of pain and stress management.
The Shealy Institute became the most successful and most cost-
effective pain clinic in the U.S, with eighty-five percent success in
more than thirty thousand patients. The Shealy protocols for management of depression, migraine, fibromyalgia, and back pain are
increasingly being integrated into hospitals and individual practices.*

*Dr. Shealy has studied the physiological effects of over a dozen
talented healers. He has demonstrated in over 116 patients that
competent healers can change the computerized electroencephalo-
gram, or brain map, from a distance and they can enhance DHEA
and beta endorphin production.*

*His current research emphasizes the potential for using elec-
tromagnetic approaches to rejuvenate the body's production of
DHEA and Calcitonin, as well as to reduce free radicals. His latest discovery is rejuvenation of DNA telomeres, which are critical
for health and longevity.*

*Dr. Shealy holds ten patents for innovative discoveries, has
published over three hundred articles and twemty-four books, the
latest of which are* Life Beyond 100: Secrets of the Fountain of
Youth *and* Soul Medicine. *In 2008* Medical Renaissance: The
Secret Code, *a movie on the benefits of Complementary and Inte-
grative Medicine, will be released. His free e-newsletter is available at* www.normshealy.com. *Holos University information is
at* www.holosuniversity.org.